God's Messengers

for Today's Women

Hearing God's Call
Through Bible Mothers

Tina Carey

To my dear friend compatriot & spiritual sister Holly: May the pilgrims full [...] with peace & joy. Love, Tina

Outskirts Press, Inc.
Denver, Colorado

God's Messengers for Today's Women
Hearing God's Call Through Bible Mothers
All Rights Reserved
Copyright © 2007 Tina Carey
V 5.0

Outskirts Press
http://www.outskirtspress.com

ISBN-10: 1-4327-0541-5
ISBN-13: 978-1-4327-0541-1

Outskirts Press and the "OP" logo are trademarks belonging to
Outskirts Press, Inc.

Printed in the United States of America

Dedication

This book is dedicated to the still small voice in all of us—that part of us waiting to rediscover the wonder, mystery and delight in all aspects of our lives.

Table of Contents

Preface

I have always felt Spirit in my life. From the time I was a small child, I felt I was protected and loved even in my loneliest times. While this feeling was constant, my religious path was quite eclectic—christened as a Catholic, divorced parents at the age of seven, went to a Baptist Sunday school, my mother married a part-time Congregational minister and somehow I went to Jewish day camp. In the summer before the 8th grade, I stayed with a family in Oklahoma where the mom was Catholic and the dad was Jewish so I practiced Catholicism during that time. I became a Presbyterian as a teenager, and as an adult, have most recently been a member of the United Methodist Church.

Through all of these organizations and periods of my life, there has always been an inner knowing, a calling of sorts from within the deepest parts of my soul. I have known it as a calling from God. This call has been the driving force in my life—sometimes more pronounced than others, and still, always there.

For me, God's call comes in many forms and from countless directions. Have you ever had a feeling you needed to do something specific that may not have been what you expected? How often have you felt pushed to call someone out of the blue? What about finding yourself in a situation that surprised you, and later you realized that something changed because of your presence? For me, these are all examples of hearing God's call and responding to that inspiration.

Do I always want to respond to the call? Not hardly. Sometimes I just want to screen the call as if I had caller ID. Even though I may feel this way, my experience has been that when the call comes, it's always easier in the end if I just answer it sooner rather than later because hearing God's call and responding in a timely manner continually puts me in the right place at the right time. For instance, in 1994 I met a woman pastor who came to speak at my church about "Living in the Spirit." During her presentation, she said something that resonated with me and reminded me of a book I had read called *The Celestine Prophecy*. This book refers to the notion that coincidence is really the evidence of God working in the world. If we can pay attention to coincidence, we will discover our spiritual path unfolding in front of us.

After her presentation, I asked her if she had read *The Celestine Prophecy* and her answer was "yes." She also shared an experience she had with a spiritual counselor, Cheryl Phillips (who has become my counselor as well). Months later, I was reminded of that conversation during an exchange I was having with my roommate. It was the combination of both conversations that led me to discover the Feminine Face of God through a series of correspondence courses (WomanSpirit Studies) with Katherine Torres. The course is called *Daughters of the Moon.*

As you are reading about my discoveries, consider episodes in your life where coincidence or "following your gut" has taken you to a surprising place of transformation for your life, or for that of someone else. For me, this is hearing and responding to God's call.

My belief system has always been broader than any particular religious course of study. Thus, when I came upon Katherine's WomanSpirit studies, they were not totally foreign to me. Initially I was a reluctant recruit. My counselor, Cheryl, encouraged me to consider the studies. I felt I wasn't ready to make a long-term commitment that required a full year to complete each level of study. Finally, I made the commitment, did the work and, deep inside, I now know, I was hearing God's call through the words of Katherine Torres.

Katherine heard her own calling in 1994 and that calling led her on a year-long spiritual journey with the Feminine Face of God – WomanSpirit. In Katherine's case, God's face was revealed with each cycle of the moon through an ancient Celtic face. Katherine calls these elements of God, the Moon Mothers.

Once I made the commitment, and began the WomanSpirit work, I moved quickly through the first two levels of *Daughters of the Moon* correspondence course. I did my studies monthly, provided my written reports, and attended a powerful retreat. When I thought about going into the final phase of the High Priestess level, I knew that part of my commitment would be to take these teachings out to the world.

Before taking the Celtic Moon Mother teachings out to the world, as a member of the United Methodist Church, I felt I needed to somehow find a bridge between my studies of WomanSpirit and the tenets of the Christian church at large. Even though I might see the Christian connection in my Celtic Moon Mother studies in my own mind, I wanted to provide a credible link based upon the teachings of the Bible since this book is the basis of religions throughout the world. In May of 2005, at a Sacred Silence retreat, I was gifted with that bridge and this book is the work that came forth.

My bridge is created through women of the Bible. I realized that for every Celtic Moon Mother of WomanSpirit, there is a woman of the Bible who embodies that same energy. The pastor that I heard in 1994 became my friend and an invaluable partner in this endeavor. Each month we worked with the values of the Bible Mothers as they related to the Celtic Moon Mother. As I probed deeper, I discovered the joy and power these women embodied in their time. I humbly bring them to you for your own study and contemplation.

I want to share another realization that came to me. In ancient times, women gathered in community with each other in search of, and in celebration of their relationship with God. Women creating community is quite common in many cultures such as the Celtic, Native American and Ancient Egyptian. This kind of community has been missing in my life and I feel certain there are women throughout the world that feel the same way. In addition to providing a meaningful link between the Bible Mothers and the Celtic Moon Mothers, it is also my vision that this book will support and encourage women to gather and study together.

Looking back at the path I have followed, I am amazed at what has been created in my life as a result of hearing God's call – and my willingness to respond to that call. I hope sharing my journey will inspire you to review your own journey, and to enjoy a new one as we rediscover the power of the women of the Judeo/Christian faiths.

Introduction

The Celtic Moon Mothers

This book can be used in conjunction with Katherine Torres' book *The Faces of WomanSpirit – A Celtic Oracle of Avalon.* It also stands on its own with the following explanation of the Celtic Moon Mothers.

It is my experience in the Christian church that God has had a male face. *God's Messengers for Today's Women* is an invitation to see the feminine face of God and to work with that re-emerging Divine Feminine Energy. In my view, both masculine and feminine energy exist and are evident all around us. I am reminded of a comment from another teacher that, "God is not a single parent."

This journey opens us to the opportunity to see and work with God through the Divine Feminine. In Katherine's work, the Divine Feminine is called "WomanSpirit." Her course of discovering the Divine Feminine was guided through each moon (month) of the year. I have learned that in studying the *Faces of WomanSpirit* through the Celtic Moon Mothers, I have an additional "lens" through which I reflect on my life. I tend to recognize patterns through this lens and gain clarity regarding various elements of my path.

Just as the earth moves through space, so does the moon and her phases. In each Celtic Moon Mother timing, you will see a reference to a sign of the Zodiac. These are fluid references since our Julian calendar only gives us 12 months when, during each "year," we actually have 13 sets of moon phases.

Study of the moon and the alignment with the various energies that come through during each moon cycle are ancient in nature and recognized by many cultures such as the Native Americans. In Katherine's work, she studies the Divine Feminine through the Celtic culture where the Celtic Moon Mothers are named for plants and trees. Their names are carried forward in this work.

The Celtic Moon Mothers represent each moon of the year and show a different element of the Feminine Face of God, or the Divine Feminine. The Divine is a complex being and the same is true for every being. Likewise, we are all a reflection of the divine in the world.

As I studied each Celtic month/moon, the unique qualities of each face of the divine were revealed to me. Because of my Christian background, I recognized there are women in the Bible who reflect and represent those same qualities connecting the two traditions in a most profound manner.

Consider the fact that these Celtic Moon Mothers give us an easier way to recognize and connect with the Divine Feminine. My work to uncover the Bible Mothers takes the opportunity to recognize the Divine Feminine into a familiar course of study known as the Bible. Most readers of this book probably were raised in the Judeo/Christian culture. This book can be used as a bridge to find the Divine Feminine revealed through the women in the Bible.

As I began to study these women of the Bible, my first realization was that there is very little joy and playfulness expressed in the stories of the women of the Bible. My belief is that is not truly factual, but the perspective of the authors and their opinion of the lives of the women of that time. In today's world, we may consider third world country women who are living in poverty to be in very sad states. With a closer look we can see that they create joy each and every day. I share this as explanation for my selections and my choice to expand on what I read as their stories.

The following table is a simple cross reference of the Celtic Moon Mothers and the Old and New Testament Bible Mothers that will serve as the road map for this book.

Celtic Moon Mother	Old Testament Bible Mother	New Testament Bible Mother
Birch	Rachel	Anna
Rowan	Tamar	Martha, Sister of Mary
Ash	Eve	Priscilla
Alder	Bathsheba	Salome, Mother of James and John
Willow	Pharaoh's Daughter	Woman of Samaria
Hawthorn	Queen Vashti	Lydia
Oak	Sarah	Elizabeth
Holly	Queen Esther	Mary Magdalene
Hazel	Ruth	Mary the Mother Jesus
Grape Vine	Queen of Sheba	Mary of Bethany
Ivy	Rahab	Unnamed Woman with the Issue of Blood
Reed	Deborah	Pilate's Wife
Elder	Hannah	Phoebe

How to Use this Book

This book is designed to be both informative and *hands on*. There are 13 chapters, one for each Celtic Moon Mother. A suggestion for working with this book is to read the book in its entirety for an overview of the Celtic Moon Mothers and the Bible Mothers. For your in-depth work which will take you over the course of a year, start with the Celtic Moon Mother that reflects your current time period. Reread that chapter and work with the meditations, Q & A's, creating your collages and key word journaling. Following is an outline with explanations of what you will find in each chapter to guide you through this inner journey.

Celtic Moon Mother Introductions

In Katherine Torres' book, *The Faces of WomanSpirit, A Celtic Oracle of Avalon*, there is an in-depth description of the Celtic Moon Mothers complete with spiritual, emotional, mental and physical references. She discusses both the empowering and challenging aspects for each Celtic Moon Mother. For the sake of this work, I choose to include a brief reference to each Moon Mother based upon her physical appearance and the qualities that she represents as an introduction to the discussion about each of the Bible Mothers.

Time of the Year for the Celtic Moon Mothers

I suggest you consider this as a year long journey. Align yourself with the movement of the moon and corresponding Bible Mothers. As I mentioned in the introduction, the timing of the Celtic Moon Mothers is based upon the 13 sets of moon phases that doesn't match completely match with our 12 month Julian calendar and

Zodiac signs. To help you find a starting point, here is an approximate guideline for you to start your journey with the Celtic Moon Mothers.

Approximate Timeline for Celtic Moon Mothers

Birch	Capricorn (Dec 22 – Jan 19)
Rowan	Aquarius (Jan 20 – Feb 18)
Ash	Pisces (Feb 19 – March 20)
Alder	Aries (March 21 – April 19)
Willow	Taurus (April 20 – May 20)
Hawthorn	Gemini (May 21 – June 21)
Oak	Cancer (June 22 – July 22)
Holly	Leo (July 23 – Aug 22)
Hazel	Virgo (Aug 23 – Sep 22)
Grape Vine	Virgo (Aug 23 – Sep 22) Libra (Sep 23 – Oct 23)
Ivy	Libra (Sept 23 – Oct 23) Scorpio (Oct 24 – Nov 21)
Reed	Scorpio (Oct 24 – Nov 21) Sagittarius (Nov 22 – Dec 21)
Elder	Sagittarius (Nov 22 – Dec 21)

Note: *For an accurate identification of which Celtic Moon Mother to start with based upon the time you are beginning, you may obtain that information on the website of Katherine Torres: www.facesofwomanspirit.com*

In your meditations, begin to bring forth images of that Bible Mother that work for you. Enhance your meditation space and time by:

- Creating a sacred place in your home where you may have quiet time each day.
- Place candles nearby, a favorite stone or necklace, and bring the images of those Bible Mothers as well.
- Use photos of one of your grandmothers, or one of the women of history you most admire—whatever image inspires the Bible Mother attributes in you. Work with them every day during that month.
- Find 15 minutes every day to begin an inner journey of faith with the Feminine Face of God.

Key Words of Empowerment

The words identified for each Celtic Moon Mother were selected because of their connection to the qualities of the Bible Mothers.

Personal Inspirations

My personal work with the empowering guidance of the Celtic Moon Mothers is shared as a tool for you to look within at your own journey to see the connections to the time of year and what is happening for you. As you travel through this year-long process, you can journal your own connections to the Celtic Moon Mothers and Bible Mothers.

Bible Mothers

For each Celtic Moon Mother, the Old Testament and New Testament Bible Mothers are identified.

Old Testament and New Testament Scriptures

These are taken from the King James Version.

Interpretations

As you read the scriptures, you will have your own interpretations of how these stories about Bible Mothers relate to the empowering qualities of the Celtic Moon Mothers. I have included my interpretations as a starting point for your personal discovery.

Guided Meditations

To prepare for each guided meditation, I invite you to first prepare yourself physically, mentally, emotionally and spiritually for your journey with the Bible Mothers. Each meditation begins with an invitation to prepare for your Spiritual Journey by first energetically "grounding" yourself. This preparation time may include:

- Turning off the phone
- Selecting soft, soothing music to play during your time with them
- Preparing the room for meditation by lighting candles, lowering the lights, lighting some incense and/or selecting a stone you enjoy holding
- Soaking and resting in the bathtub
- Quieting your mind

You may want to spend a few minutes in quiet contemplation, focused only on your breath and allowing yourself to enter a deep peaceful state. This may be a time of prayer and contemplation for you. Once you have completed your own preparation and have found a peaceful state, you are ready for your journey.

Question and Answer Worksheets

Taking a concept beyond the intellectual process and putting it into a kinetic experience helps to imprint the information deeper into the consciousness. The question and answer worksheets provide you with thought provoking ideas to further immerse yourself into the inspirations of the Bible Mothers.

Bible Mother Images

Initially it was my intention to provide Bible Mother images at the end of each chapter. Through my spiritual journey in the writing of the book, I realized that each of us has our own image or images of these women. As you work with each Bible Mother pair, I invite you to find the images to which you relate.

The images may be from famous artists such as DaVinci or Mary Cassatt. You may find inspiration through various card decks such as Amy Sophia Marishinsky's *Oracle of the Grail Code* or decks by Doreen Virtue. Women of recent history– Jackie Kennedy, Eleanor Roosevelt or Mother Theresa may be selections. You may find the inspiration from women of your own family! Think of the treasure you have at your finger tips in family albums, for example.

There is a page for you to make a collage of your Bible Mother images. Enjoy this powerful process and let your imagination go!

Key Word Journal Pages

As you travel through your time with the Bible Mothers, these sheets are to trigger your memory and capture examples where your life has reflected examples of these key words of empowerment.

Getting Started

Creating Your Inner Sanctuary

The first step for preparing to work in the inner worlds where all these Mothers (Celtic and Bible) can be accessed is to create that sacred, safe place inside you. This is the place where all inner exploration can begin—your inner sanctuary.

Your Perfect Place

Consider this an opportunity to dream about your perfect place – a cottage by the beach, a cabin in the mountains, a castle in the sky – let your imagination lead you. Find a picture that represents this place. It might be in a magazine or something you can print off the web. Just start with the image of your dream place. Once you have the image, try this guided meditation:

- *Study your house in silence.*
- *Close your eyes.*
- *Imagine standing in front of your house.*
- *Where is it?*
- *What type of land is it on?*
- *Is it in the forest?*
- *On the beach?*
- *In a meadow?*

- *Note the outside surroundings.*
- *Walk up to the door.*
- *Reach for the door knob – it's open – for you.*
- *Walk in.*
- *Notice the living room you've entered.*
- *How big is it?*
- *What kind of furniture is there?*
- *What is on the walls?*
- *How many windows?*
- *Get comfortable with the room and go exploring.*
- *How many other rooms are in the house?*
- *What do they look like?*
- *What colors do you see in each room?*
- *What kind of furniture?*
- *Visualize the entire inside of the cottage.*
- *Fill in all the spaces with your imagination.*
- *There is one special place within your house– the place you have created to be your personal inner sanctuary.*
- *Find that place.*
- *What does the room look like?*
- *Do you have any windows?*
- *What color are the walls, curtains?*
- *Look at the furniture– is there any or is it an empty space?*
- *What does the floor look like?*
- *Find your personal sacred table.*
- *What do you find on it?*
- *List all the items you find, take note of all the special sacred items you find. Is there...*
  - a candle?

- a stone or shell?

- a photograph or picture?

- a statue or toy?

- a perfume bottle?

- *Now take a walk out back and see the rest of the picture.*
- *Become familiar with your special place, the land, the neighborhood—the whole environment.*
- *It is a place of comfort, peace, relaxation – a place for you to recharge.*

Your Visual Image

Now you have seen your Inner Sanctuary. Take this opportunity to create a visual image of this special place.

1. List all the elements you saw in your house. You can list them, draw them, create a collage – what ever works for you to remember how that new house looks and feels to you.
2. Pay careful attention to the sacred sanctuary room and table and list those items you found in that room.
3. What are the elements you saw in your sacred space?
4. What do they represent to you?
5. Why are these items special?
6. What meaning do they have for you?

Your Personal Altar

Now that you have created a collage, and captured the essence of you Inner Sanctuary, you can also create a personal altar containing the sacred elements you found in your Inner Sanctuary. What we visualize in the inner heart, we create in the outer world. The peace, freedom and warmth that you feel within your inner sanctuary is represented by your personal altar and the elements you have collected. They become a door to access your Inner Sanctuary and are available to you all the time! I bring portable elements with me when I travel. You can carry them or a symbol of them in your pocket or purse.

Your Inner Journey

When preparing for an inner journey, you can begin from your Inner Sanctuary. You can access your Inner Sanctuary from anywhere—home, the bath tub, the beach, on a plane, in the office—just bring the image of your collage to your mind and walk through the door.

BIRCH ◈ BETH

©1997 Katherine Torres, Ph. D., Transpersonal Development

Birch Celtic Moon Mother

She expresses purity and potential. Her bridal veil, flowers and feathers represent new patterns being formed and new beginnings. These are her gifts after honoring the sacred silence of Elder. Her face is flecked with snowflakes, each sparkle reveals a spectrum of light and once in awhile, reveal color (potentials to be realized). Her ice-blue eyes reveal her ability to see the prospective events even in the starkest realities.

Time of Year

Birch reflects the power of the sun in Capricorn. She is the first light after the dark night of winter. She expresses her radiant light at Winter Solstice.

Key Words of Empowerment

- Purity, Potential
- Setting goals
- Cutting old cords
- Gestation, dream work
- Patience, Observe
- Focus

Personal Inspiration

Patience/Focus—Birch was a time for finding financial solutions for my in-laws. Rather than taking over their mortgage and quickly solving the situation, I discovered that they could do a reverse mortgage. I was able to share my learning with my sister-in-law and she became the facilitator for her parents. My patience and seed planting resulted in a better choice for all involved.

Cutting Old Cords/Gestation—During the time of Birch, I planted the seeds for appropriate action for my son. As it happens too often in these times, his relationship with the mother of his child was not very positive. He needed financial support to formalize his parental rights for his daughter. We had planted the seeds of resolution by ensuring appropriate legal counsel and an earlier paternity test. As a result, he received joint custody of his beautiful daughter—who was born in the time of Birch.

Bible Mothers for Birch Celtic Moon Mother

Old Testament – Rachel

New Testament – Anna

Birch Bible Mother—Old Testament

Rachel

Scripture: Genesis 29:9-12, 16-18, 20-21, 23, 25-27, 30

While he was still talking with them, Rachel came with her father's sheep, for she was a shepherdess. When Jacob saw Rachel daughter of Laban, his mother's brother, and Laban's sheep, he went over and rolled the stone away from the mouth of the well and watered his uncle's sheep. Then Jacob kissed Rachel and began to weep aloud. He had told Rachel that he was a relative of her father and a son of Rebekah. So she ran off and told her father.

Now Laban had two daughters; the name of the older was Leah, and the name of the younger was Rachel. Leah had weak eyes, but Rachel was lovely in form, and beautiful. Jacob was in love with Rachel and said, "I'll work for you for seven years in return for your youngest daughter Rachel."

So Jacob served seven years to get Rachel, but they seemed like only a few days to him because of his love for her.

Then Jacob said to Laban, "Give me my wife. My time is completed, and I want to lie with her."

But when evening came, he took his daughter Leah and gave her to Jacob, and Jacob lay with her.

When morning came, there was Leah! So Jacob said to Laban, "What is this you have done to me? I served you for Rachel, didn't I? Why have you deceived me?"

Laban replied, "It is not our custom here to give the younger daughter in marriage before the older one. Finish this daughter's bridal week; then we will give you the younger one also, in return for another seven years of work."

Jacob lay with Rachel also, and he loved Rachel more than Leah. And he worked for Laban another seven years.

When Rachel saw that she was not bearing Jacob any children, she became jealous of her sister. So she said to Jacob, "Give me children, or I'll die!"

Jacob became angry with her and said, "Am I in the place of God, who has kept you from having children?"

Then God remembered Rachel; he listened to her and opened her womb. She became pregnant and gave birth to a son and said, "God has taken away my disgrace." She named him Joseph, and said, "May the Lord add to me another son."

Interpretation

Herbert Lockyer in *Women of the Bible* describes Rachel as "The woman in whom romance and tragedy were blended." This description captures the essence of the patience required for her romance to be fulfilled.

Rachel was a woman of great **patience.** It is clear from the beginning of the story that her love for Jacob was great. She endured waiting seven years and then lost him to her sister. She finally prevailed and married Jacob, but it cost him an additional seven years in service to her father.

In her book, *Women in the Old Testament*, Irene Nowell describes Rachel's patience and continued planning to create first her marriage with Jacob and eventually create her children with him.

Rachel was a great planner and a woman of **clear goals.** She first wanted to marry the man she loved and then wanted to have children with him. She planned, prayed and waited patiently for her dreams to come to fruition, and they did. Her son, Joseph, became the favored child of Jacob, the son of his great love.

Birch Bible Mother—New Testament
Anna

Scripture: Luke 2:36-38

There was also a prophetess, Anna, the daughter of Phanuel, of the tribe of Asher. She was very old; she had lived with her husband seven years after her marriage, and then was a widow until she was eighty-four. She never left the temple but worshipped night and day, fasting and praying. Coming up to them at that very moment, she gave thanks to God and spoke about the child to all who were looking for ward to the redemption of Jerusalem.

Interpretation

Anna was a woman of true **discipline** and **discernment.** Herbert Lockyer in *Women in the Bible* tells us she was a prophetess – meaning she proclaimed a divine message. She was widowed after only seven years, and chose, at that time to become one of "the band of holy women" and was in constant attendance in the temple. She spent her later years secluded in the temple in constant prayer and worship. She was an observer of life within the temple, and paid attention to those coming and going in their work and worship.

Mary Ann Getty-Sullivan in *Women in the New Testament* gives us a hint of the longing in Anna – that longing for the promised Messiah. In the process, within herself, she was open to the new dream of the changes to come and developed the voice to speak the truth as she saw it. It took preparation and willingness to recognize the child, Jesus, for who he was and who he was to be.

Birch Bible Mother Meditation
Rachel and Anna

You are seated in a space of morning light. Visualize an anchor of light coming from the top of your head down through your feet and hooking into the core of the earth. Breathe deeply sending energy down this cord and see it coming back up into your being.

Two women greet you in the early morning light. One has come in from the fields and flocks and is a true beauty. She has auburn hair and bright green eyes. She smiles in greeting and brings you a blessing with a gift in her hands. It is a small doll made of straw that fits in your hands. Behind her you see an older woman in a robe and hood. Her blue eyes sparkle as she greets you. Her gift is a simple cord she hands you, to tie around your own waist.

Rachel and Anna lead you to a space near a softly running brook. There is a grassy spot where you can rest. They ask you, "What are your dreams? What are your goals for your life?" They share with you the fact that your words are very powerful and encourage you to write down the dreams you have articulated to help you to energize them. They invite you to take them with you as you return to your room.

Rachel and Anna Worksheet

1. *As you met Rachel and Anna, did you recognize them? Who did they resemble?*

2. *What does the doll look like that you were given? Did you ever have a doll like this one?*

3. *What color is the cord you were given? What does it represent?*

4. *What dreams did you share?*

Tina Carey

Images of Bible Mothers
Rachel and Anna

Key Word Journal for Bible Mothers
Rachel and Anna

Key Words of Empowerment

- Purity, Potential
- Setting goals
- Cutting old cords
- Gestation, dream work
- Patience, Observe
- Focus

ROWAN · LUIS

© 1997 Katherine Torres, Ph. D., Transpersonal Development

Rowan Celtic Moon Mother

She expresses the first signs of winter ending its hold on the cycle of the year. The flowers on her face present hope for the fresh new days of light. Her eyes are dotted with tiny little flowers—the promise of dreams unfolding. Over her third eye she carries the design of a diamond shape. It is the power of truth, the essence of deliberate focus and the quality of a vehicle of light that will take you through dynamic changes of the Universe.

of Year

Rowan reflects the power of the sun in Aquarius.

Key Words of Empowerment

- Dreams unfolding
- Diligent, deliberate
- Direct, Truth
- Un-swaying
- Graceful
- Intelligence, Intent
- Purpose, Independent
- Doing without outcome
- Doing things differently

Personal Inspiration

Doing things differently—For me, Rowan brings times of changing my behaviors. One year I was working on a project in Las Vegas for a client when I received a phone message that my former mother-in-law had been in a car accident. My behavior in the past would have been to catch the next plane and be there in person for her. I could have flown back within an hour and gotten to the hospital to take care of things. This time, I didn't. I called her daughter and I allowed the family to "be of service to her" instead of me.

Graceful—In 2006, I flew to Arizona to help my friend Nita Moffitt after she had surgery. It was a wonderful time of reflection and support. One afternoon we drove to a beautiful spot called the Shrine of St. Joseph in a tiny Arizona town to experience a spiritual walk carved into the hillside there. Nita and I spent the morning walking in that shrine and reflecting on the various images in the hillside. It was her first outing after her surgery—a time together that was full of grace.

Direct/Truth/Unswaying—This was also a time for me to return to visit my step-sister, Ginna Sue, and give her a Reiki healing one more time before her passing. Prior to going to see her, I had a very direct conversation with her reminding her that I was coming to support her rather than to be entertained, and to insist that I was coming.

Diligent/Deliberate—During the time of Rowan, I decided to host a "baby blessing" in honor of my granddaughter at my new home. I created a ritual for the baby blessing. First, I placed index cards in a basket. Each card had an attribute written on it (i.e.) beauty, friendship, joy, etc. Next, everyone at the gathering was invited to come forward and bless my granddaughter with their words and then sprinkle her toes with "fairy dust." Rowan's energy invites us to take deliberate action based upon our truth as we know it regardless what others might think.

Bible Mothers for Rowan Celtic Moon
Old Testament – Tamar
New Testament – Martha, Sister of Mary

Rowan Bible Mother—Old Testament
Tamar

Scripture: Genesis 38:6-19, 24-26

Judah got a wife for Er, his firstborn, and her name was Tamar. Bur Er, Judah's firstborn, was wicked in the Lord's sight; so the Lord put him to death.

Then Judah said to Onan, "Lie with your brother's wife and fulfill your duty to her as a brother-in-law to produce offspring for your brother." But Onan knew that the offspring would not be his; so whenever he lay with his brother's wife, he spilled his semen on the ground to keep from producing an offspring for his brother. What he did was wicked in the Lord's sight; so he put him to death also.

Judah then said to his daughter-in-law Tamar, "Live as a widow in your father's house until my son Shelah grows up." For he thought "He may die, too, just like his brothers." So Tamar went to live in her father's house.

After a long time Judah's wife died. When Judah had recovered from his grief, he went to Timnah.

When Tamar was told, "Your father-in-law is on his way to Timnah to shear his sheep," she took off her widow's clothes, covered herself with a veil to disguise herself, and then sat down at the entrance to Enaim, which is on the road to Timnah. For she saw that, though Shelah had now grown up, she had not been given to him as his wife.

When Judah saw her, he thought she was a prostitute, for she had covered her face. Not realizing that she was his daughter-in-law, he went over to her by the roadside and said, "Come now, let me sleep with you."

"And what will you give me to sleep with you?" she asked.

"I'll send you a young goat from my flock," he said.

"Will you give me something as a pledge until you send it?" she asked.

He said, "What pledge should I give you?"

"Your seal and its cord, and the staff in your hand," she answered. So he gave them to her and slept with her, and she became pregnant by him. After she left, she took off her veil and put on her widow's clothes again.

About three months later Judah was told, "Your daughter-in-law Tamar is guilty of prostitution, and as a result she is now pregnant."

Judah said, "Bring her out and have her burned to death!"

As she was being brought out, she sent a message to her father-in-law, "I am pregnant by the man who owns these," she said. And she added, "See if you recognize whose seal and cord and staff these are."

Judah recognized them and said, "She is more righteous than I, since I wouldn't give her to my son Shelah." And he did not sleep with her again.

Interpretation

Tamar was a woman willing to use her logic to save herself. She is also an important link and a direct ancestor of Jesus. Her importance is reflected in her placement within the book of Genesis as shared by Helen Bruch Pearson in *Mother Roots*. She was **diligent** and **deliberate** in her actions and was able to create a meaningful life for herself and her children. She used the elements of deliberate focus to create an escape. Herbert Lockyer reflects in *Women of the Bible* that Tamar was motivated by noble motives—to become the mother of Judah's tribal representative.

Tamar is a woman who created her own future by thinking, planning, focusing and in the end, manifesting the freedom and security she required for her own survival. Her planning and her ability to weave her story tied Judah to her energetically. Although he would not marry her or have her marry his son, she survived.

Rowan Bible Mother—New Testament
Martha, Sister of Mary

Scripture: Luke 10:38-41

As Jesus and his disciples were on their way, he came to a village where a woman named Martha opened her home to him. She had a sister called Mary, who sat at the Lord's feet listening to what he had said. But Martha was distracted by all the preparations that had to be made. She came to him and asked, "Lord, don't you care that my sister has left me to do the work by myself? Tell her to help me!"

"Martha, Martha," the Lord answered, "You are worried and upset about many things, but only one thing is needed. Mary has chosen what is better, and it will not be taken away from her."

Interpretation

Martha is a perfect image of Rowan—logical, practical, **deliberate**, and stubborn. Herbert Lockyer in *Women of the Bible* describes her as the woman who was more practical than spiritual. She is the planner, the doer, and the keeper of the house and does find a way to speak her truth, even though she feels rebuked by Jesus. Nell W. Mahoney in *From Mary to Lydia* describes Martha as the right-brain thinker. She struggles with the idea of silent contemplation and feel the need to be "doing."

Mary Ann Getty-Sullivan in *Women in the New Testament* adds the texture of the needs of the early church for women who are doers—those of deliberate focus—to ensure the practical needs of the new communities continue to be met.

We have thought of Martha, in most cases, as the sister who missed the point of Jesus' visit. Yet, she maintained deliberate focus of her task at hand. Martha's intention to create the perfect environment would have required incredible planning and deliberate focus to the task at hand. These are elements we must celebrate within all women. **Deliberate** focus takes hard work and Martha is that hidden, practical side of all women, similar to Martha Stewart who is creative, deliberate, a master planner and a great **story teller**. Martha is the energy behind the scene, creating an elegant gathering for her guests. This is also true of Martha of the Bible and these are all elements of Celtic Moon Mother Rowan.

Rowan Bible Mother Meditation
Tamar and Martha, Sister of Mary

You are seated in a space of afternoon light. Visualize an anchor of light coming from the top of your head down through your feet and hooking into the core of the earth. Breathe deeply sending energy down this cord and see it coming back up into your being.

You are seated in a rocker next to a cheerfully burning fireplace in a cozy kitchen. You see, at the stove, Martha preparing a meal. Seated on the hearth is Tamar. These two practical women are here to help you find the logical path to move your goals forward. Martha finishes at the stove, takes off her apron, hangs it over a chair next to you and pulls up a stool beside the rocker.

She and Tamar begin to ask you about your dreams. What is next? What steps can they help you with planning and putting action items together? How real does your dream feel? They ask you to tell them the story of your new life and the dream you have manifested. You pour out the details and begin to see the new future laid out before you. Tamar and Martha view that new future with you and the three of you together breathe into that picture your new life. Tamar hands you a sacred seal created just for you, and Martha hands you a yummy snack to sustain you before they bring you back to your room.

Tamar and Martha Worksheet

1. *When you met Tamar and Martha, did you recognize them? If so, who are they?*

2. *What kind of meal did Martha prepare?*

3. *What did your new future look like?*

4. *What happened when you breathed into it with Tamar and Martha?*

Tina Carey

Images of Bible Mothers
Tamar and Martha

Key Word Journal for Bible Mothers
Tamar and Martha

Key Words of Empowerment

- Dreams unfolding
- Diligent, deliberate
- Direct, Truth
- Un-swaying
- Graceful
- Intelligence, Intent
- Purpose, Independent
- Doing without outcome
- Doing things differently

ASH ✦ NION

Ash Celtic Moon Mother

She signifies the beauty of Spring Equinox and its gracious call to balance through her black and white color. The moon and stars upon her face indicate internal and external guidance. Her eyes are soft blue, the color of ocean water and the reflective power of wisdom. Her face holds secret coding of intuitive and supernatural powers.

23

Time of Year

Ash reflects the power of the sun in Pisces and its movement toward Alder.

Key Words of Empowerment

- Divine Feminine expression, ancient wisdom
- Practice of compassion
- Knower, sensitive
- Dedicated to serve, respect
- Influential, Humble
- Ritual, Magic
- Making Holy

Personal Inspiration

Ancient wisdom/Ritual/Magic—Ash brings a time of access to ancient wisdom as well as an invitation to create new ritual and magic to make one's life experience holy. My time with Ash includes a lot of inner work as well as time of service to others and the world. For example, one year in meditation, I was invited to look at all the men in my life who had disappointed me. There had been lots of them. In fact, at the time, I had trouble thinking of one man in my life that I truly respected.

As I continued to contemplate this fact, I realized that part of the problem was actually coming from within me. My experience has been that what I feel inside myself gets reflected in my outside world. I realized that these men were reflecting back to me what I was expecting of them. I was expecting the worst instead of the best. In my meditation, I created a ritual to allow my inner self to step up first by visualizing that "male" self inside. I looked at him as he stood in front of me and allowed him to "be fully present" with integrity and authenticity. Once I completed the inner work, I realized that I could look to the men in my life to begin doing the same.

Practice of Compassion—One year, during the time of Ash, I had a very emotional experience when my step-sister, Ginna Sue, died. This brought a time of great ritual for me in her memorial service. I was asked to sing three songs at the service. I got through the first two and while singing the third, *The Wind Beneath My Wings*, I totally lost it. My son said to me later, "Mom, NO ONE could have gotten through that song! What were you thinking?" What happened energetically was quite remarkable. In this time of deep ritual of remembrance, nearly 300 people were all holding onto their emotions very tightly. When I began to cry, it was as if a wave of emotion moved through the crowd and the magic of emotional release was complete.

Bible Mothers for Ash Celtic Moon
   Old Testament – Eve
   New Testament – Priscilla

Ash Bible Mother—Old Testament
Eve

Scripture: Genesis 3:2-7

The woman said to the serpent, "We may eat fruit from the trees in the garden, but God did say, 'You must not eat fruit from the tree that is in the middle of the garden, and you must not touch it, or you will die.'"

"You will surely not die," the serpent said to the woman. "For God knows that when you eat of it, your eyes will be opened, and you will be like God, knowing good and evil."

When the woman saw that the fruit of the tree was good for food and pleasing to the eye, and also desirable for gaining wisdom, she took some and ate it. She also gave some to her husband who was with her, and he ate it. Then the eyes of both of them were opened.

Interpretation

Herbert Lockyer gives Eve an evocative title—The Woman of Unique Distinction. She is the product of a divine creation. She appeared as a complete, perfect woman. As such, Eve is, in this story, hungry for knowledge and wisdom of the spirit. It is through her quest for wisdom that our spiritual nature is revealed – the wisdom to know the difference between illusion and truth and the gift of truly being part of the divine.

Her story is a reminder that we are truly spiritual beings having a human experience. Eve looked through the illusion of fear to the gift and the sacrifice of knowledge that the apple would bring in the form of clear vision.

Eve is a humble and sensitive person looking for ways to serve the highest good in the garden. She personifies the feminine in her curiosity and willingness to look beyond the current barriers to the potential and responsibility of true knowledge and magic. Her magic is the transformation and opening of her eyes to the greater mysteries of life and, through her, the eyes of all humanity.

Ash Bible Mother—New Testament
Priscilla

Scripture: Acts 18:1-3, 24-26

After this, Paul left Athens and went to Corinth. There he met a Jew named Aquila a native of Pontus, who had recently come from Italy with his wife Priscilla, because Claudius had ordered all the Jews to leave Rome. Paul went to see them, and because he was a tent maker as they were, he stayed and worked with them.

Meanwhile a Jew named Apollos, a native of Alexandria, came to Ephesus. He was a learned man, with a thorough knowledge of the Scriptures. He had been instructed in the way of the Lord, and he spoke with great fervor and taught about Jesus accurately, though he knew only the baptism of John. He began to speak boldly in the synagogue. When Priscilla and Aquila heard him, they invited him to their home and explained to him the way of God more adequately.

Interpretation

Nell W. Mahoney in *From Mary to Lydia* notes that Priscilla is a servant leader with a keen mind and loving heart. These short passages reveal her as a **heart centered** woman. When she is present to hear the preaching of Apollos, she recognizes the illusion in his words. Both Herbert Lockyer in *Women in the Bible* and Nell W. Mahoney in *From Mary to Lydia* refer to this realization. She is **humble** in her outreach to Apollos and is willing to share her **wisdom** and eliminate the illusion under which she operates.

Priscilla is also an influential leader within her community and continues to express the beauty of the feminine through her telling of the stories of Jesus. She is truly **dedicated to serve** in all ways.

Priscilla, like Eve, looks beyond the illusion of fear being preached by Apollos to the core truth of spirit and the transformational energy of love she perceived through the teachings of Jesus.

Ash Bible Mother Meditation
Eve and Priscilla

You are seated in a space of warm twilight. Visualize an anchor of light coming from the top of your head down through your feet and hooking into the core of the earth. Breathe deeply sending energy down this cord and see it coming back up into your being.

You are in a beautiful garden seated on a white bench. On one side of you is a beautiful woman with olive skin and brown hair. Her brown eyes twinkle at you as she smiles. Her dress is simple brown muslin and her feet are bare. On the other side of you is a blonde woman with green eyes. She is shy, but powerful in her own way. They invite you to join them in a ritual to bring in the Divine Feminine within you.

The three of you rise and hold hands to form a circle. Eve brings an apple to the center of the circle, Priscilla brings a tent stake and you look in your inner pocket and bring your own offering. You clasp hands again, visualizing a golden ball of light descending from the heavens into the center of the circle. The light expands, permeating all parts of your body, and reaching into all areas of your existence, including physical, mental, emotional and spiritual. The energy is warm, soft and inviting. You feel pampered and loved in its glow. The three of you each speak your words of welcome and thanks to the Divine Feminine. You express gratitude for the gift of life and the opportunity of the spiritual journey. The light bursts forth through you and dissipates into the ground.

Eve and Priscilla bring you back to your room with the memory of the opportunity to create ritual.

Eve and Priscilla Worksheet

1. *Who did you see when you met Eve and Priscilla?*

2. *How did it feel to join these women in a circle?*

3. *What offering did you find in your inner pocket?*

4. *What reminder of the Divine Feminine can you take with you into the world?*

Tina Carey

Images of Bible Mothers
Eve and Priscilla

Key Word Journal for Bible Mothers
Eve and Priscilla

Key Words of Empowerment

- Divine Feminine Expression, ancient wisdom
- Practice of compassion
- Knower, sensitive
- Dedicated to serve, respect
- Influential, Humble
- Ritual, Magic
- Making holy

ALDER ✦ FEARN

Alder Celtic Moon Mother

She signifies the passion of spring and the urgency of youth to get moving. The snakes on her face call her to know the power within and use it to express herself to the world. They are indigo blue and turquoise to reveal her intent and desire to follow the path of the true will. Her eyes are the orange of delight and innocence. The flower is prepared to receive energy while the stem reveals the power to take creative action.

Time of Year

Alder reflects the power of the sun in Aries and the refreshing light of spring.

Key Words of Empowerment

- Urgency
- Bright, Intense
- Energetic, goal oriented
- No fear
- Initiator
- Delegator
- Risk taker

Personal Inspiration

Risk Taker—During the time of Alder, Mystic Sisters (my bookstore) actually took a booth at a Healing Expo in Pasadena. This was a big step for us. In addition to having a booth, I also coordinated two days of Reiki treatments in a separate location within the convention center. This resulted in expansion of our focus into the community as well as expansion of healing potentials within the community. We enlisted 7 healers to serve over those two days and we treated over 30 people

Initiator—In the time of Alder, I took the risk of creating a video presentation for one of my programs, "Organizational Resilience." It was a leap of faith to take the time and energy to create the presentation and provide a format that could be shared with a broader audience.

Bible Mothers for Alder Celtic Moon

Old Testament – Bathsheba

New Testament – Salome, Mother of James and John

Alder Bible Mother—Old Testament
Bathsheba

Scripture: II Samuel 11:2-3, 26-27

One evening David got up from his bed and walked around on the roof of the palace. From the roof he saw a woman bathing. The woman was very beautiful, and David sent someone to find out about her. The man said, "Isn't this Bathsheba, the daughter of Eliam and the wife of Uriah the Hittite?" Then David sent messengers to get her. She came to him and he slept with her. (She had purified herself from her uncleanliness.) Then the woman went back home. The woman conceived and sent word to David, saying, "I am pregnant."

When Uriah's wife heard that her husband was dead, she mourned him. After the time of mourning was over, David had her brought to his house, and she became his wife and bore him a son.

Interpretation

Bathsheba was a woman who was willing to "go for it." Helen Bruch Pearson describes her in *Mother Roots* as a woman who "beat the odds." She had a connection with David that was beyond her own understanding and she was willing to take the risk of being with him. It cost her, but she felt the risk and loss were worth it. The ultimate result of her love of David was the birth of their son, Solomon. Herbert Lockyer describes Bathsheba's transformation at this point of her life into a queen of courage and grace. She also retained influence over David throughout his life, ensuring her son, Solomon, would become successor for David's throne.

Bathsheba runs forward toward her **goal**, relentless and willing to take all risks. These are the elements of Alder and the results can be painful, as Bathsheba sees in the death of her husband, Uriah, and the loss of her first son with David. Does she regret her **energy**, her passion and her goal? Not likely.

Alder Bible Mother—New Testament
Salome, Mother of James and John

Scripture: Matthew 20:20-23

Then the mother of Zebedee's sons came to Jesus with her sons and, kneeling down, asked a favor of him.

"What is it you want?" he asked.

She said, "Grant that one of these two sons of mine may sit at your right and the other at your left in your kingdom."

"You don't know what you are asking," Jesus said to them. "Can you drink the cup I am going to drink?"

"We can," they answered.

Jesus said to them, "You will indeed drink from my cup, but to sit at my right or left is not for me to grant. Those places belong to those for whom they may have been prepared by my Father."

Interpretation

Salome is a "go for it" mom when it comes to her sons. Herbert Lockyer in *Women in the Bible* describes her as "the woman who wanted the best for her sons." She was, from the beginning, a faithful follower of Jesus. As Lockyer states, she encouraged her sons to follow him and clearly felt led to be at his mother's side during his crucifixion.

In *Women in the New Testament* by Mary Ann-Getty-Sullivan, Salome was one of the women at the crucifixion, but also at the tomb at the time of the resurrection. She knew who Jesus was and chose to ask special placement for her sons. She displays the essence of Alder Celtic Moon Mother through her determined goal to achieve the best for her sons.

She shows **determination** and **willingness** to risk anger, not only of Jesus, but of the other disciples and perhaps even her sons, to ask for what she feels they deserve. She likely participated in prayerful preparation before approaching Jesus, but decided the risk was worth it.

Alder Bible Mother Meditation

Bathsheba and Salome, Mother of James and John

You are seated in a space of evening light. Visualize an anchor of light coming from the top of your head down through your feet and hooking into the core of the earth. Breathe deeply sending energy down this cord and see it coming back up into your being.

You are at the start of a unique obstacle course of sorts. You are dressed in gym shorts, t-shirt, socks and tennis shoes. Next to you on the starting line are two women. Bathsheba is tall and lanky with her hair pulled up in a pony tail, and she is carrying a baton for a relay race. Salome is shorter and stocky, with short hair framing her face. She is carrying a whistle on a chain around her neck. Both women hand you their gifts. You may use the whistle when you become too tired and pass the baton to the next woman you meet on the course. They huddle with you to pass on their coaching advice and send you on your way.

Their energy flies with you down the course as you leap across ponds, climb rope ladders, scramble under tunnels and jump up and over walls. You can hear their encouraging cheers of "just do it!" and "go for it!" You can see the end of the track just ahead and they are holding the finish line tape for you. You blast through, exhausted and thrilled with the ride.

Salome and Bathsheba accompany you back to your room and leave with you their gifts of encouragement.

Bathsheba and Salome,
Mother of James and John Worksheet

1. *When you met Bathsheba and Salome, did you recognize them? Who do they resemble?*

2. *As you started your obstacle course, how did you feel? Ready? Panicked?*

3. *What gift did the women bring for you?*

4. *What was their coaching advice?*

Images of Bible Mothers

Bathsheba and Salome, Mother of James and John

Key Word Journal for Bible Mothers
Bathesheba and Salome, Mother of James and John

Key Words of Empowerment

- Urgency
- Bright, Intense
- Energetic, goal oriented
- No fear
- Initiator
- Delegator
- Risk taker

WILLOW ⟷ SAILLE

©1997 Katherine Torres, Ph. D., Transpersonal Development

Willow Celtic Moon Mother

She signifies the power of spring to renew and recover your soul. Willow's face reminds you of growth and nurturing powers. Her green eyes bring out the creative power of vision and growth. The bright yellow around her eyes is a reminder for you to stay focused during a tenuous time of birthing your desires. White flowers of purity, and green leaves of creativity and abundance, surround her soft, gentle expression.

Time of Year

Willow reflects the power of the sun in Taurus and the essence of Beltane.

Key Words of Empowerment

- Planting seeds
- Renewal, Nurturing
- Cultivation
- Expectation
- Perseverance, concentration
- Earth connection, grounding wisdom
- Illusion/reality

Personal Inspiration

Illusion/Reality—I was at a basketball game with my sons, their father and my former father-in-law at a local college. Just as the game ended, a rather large group of people began running across the gym in front of us. I felt a pervasive wave of fear all around me.

I knew my father-in-law could not run, so I just held onto him. We heard rumors of a gun either inside the gym or a shooting in the parking lot. People were running wildly. I could not see where all these people could possibly be going even though I had clear vision from where we were seated. The morning papers featured a story about an argument and a shooting outside the gym. A man had been wounded. Looking back on the situation, I saw some illusions in the event—everyone running with nowhere to go and in all the pandemonium, no one fell which typically we can expect otherwise. Recognizing we did not have to get caught up in these illusions of fear, we sat and allowed the chaos to go on around us without getting into it.

Perseverance/Concentration/Illusion/Reality—In 2005, I was on a Sacred Silence Retreat during the time of Willow when I received the inspiration to write this book.

As I described in the preface, part of my commitment to the work of the High Priestess in the *Daughters of the Moon* was to bring the information of the Feminine Face of God to the world. As I originally mentioned, I was concerned about how I could bridge the information of the Moon Mothers into my Christian foundation. It was during this time of Willow that I was able to see through the illusion of my fear from my Christian foundation, and recognize the reality that all the elements of the Feminine Divine are truly one.

Earth Connection—During the time of Willow, I was co-leading a Women's Retreat. During this retreat we used a wonderful chorale reading entitled "I Was Born Connected." This was so appropriate for Willow in it's themes of connection and recognizing the illusion of our lives because we have always been connected and always will be long after our death.

Bible Mothers for Willow Celtic Moon
   Old Testament—Pharaoh's Daughter
   New Testament – Woman of Samaria

Willow Bible Mother—Old Testament
Pharaoh's Daughter

Scripture: Exodus 1:22, 2:1-10

Then Pharaoh gave this order to all his people: "Every boy that is born you must throw into the Nile, but let every girl live."

Now a man of the house of Levi married a Levite woman, and she became pregnant and gave birth to a son. When she saw that he was a fine child, she hid him for three moths. But when she could hide him no longer, she got a papyrus basket for him and coated it with tar and pitch. Then she placed the child in it and put it among the reeds along the bank of the Nile. His sister stood at a distance to see what would happen to him.

The Pharaoh's daughter went down to the Nile to bathe, and her attendants were walking along the river bank. She saw the basket among the reeds and sent her slave girl to get it. She opened it and saw the baby. He was crying, and she felt sorry for him. "This is one of the Hebrew babies," she said.

Then his sister asked Pharaoh's daughter, "Shall I go and get one of the Hebrew women to nurse the baby for you?"

"Yes, go," she answered. And the girl went and got the baby's mother. Pharaoh's daughter said to her, "Take this baby and nurse him for me, and I will pay you." So the woman took the baby and nursed him. When the child grew older, she took him to Pharaoh's daughter and he became her son. She named him Moses, saying, "I drew him out of the water."

Interpretation

Herbert Lockyer provides an interesting slant to this story in *Women in the Bible*. As an Egyptian woman, she enjoyed great liberty and had come with her attendants to a private part of the Nile to bathe. It is there she finds what she knows to be a Hebrew baby boy in the bulrushes. Irene Nowell in her work, *Women in the Old Testament,* describes her subtle defiance in this way, "The way to break oppression is to refuse to be oppressed."

Pharaoh's daughter was a woman who followed her intuition. She was confronted with an unexpected choice and her feminine side, her mothering side, won out. She became a **nurturing** element in the life of Moses and was **connected** energetically to the rest of the women in the story. She bought into the **illusion** created in the story of the bulrushes baby and followed her heart in taking in that baby. Her action planted the seeds of a great nation and a transformation in the future that would change the world in which she lived.

Willow Bible Mother—New Testament
Woman of Samaria

Scripture: John 4:4-26

Now he had to go through Samaria. So he came to a town in Samaria called Sychar, near the plot of ground Jacob had given to his son Joseph. Jacob's well was there, and Jesus, tired as he was from the journey, sat down by the well. It was about the sixth hour.

When a Samaritan woman came to draw water, Jesus said to her, "Will you give me a drink?" (His disciples had gone into town to buy food.)

The Samaritan woman said to him, "You are a Jew and I am a Samaritan woman. How can you ask me for a drink?" (For Jews do not associate with Samaritans.)

Jesus answered her, "If you knew the gift of God and who it is that asks you for a drink, you would have asked him and he would have given you living water."

"Sir," the woman said, "you have nothing to draw with and the well is deep. Where can you get this living water? Are you greater than our father Jacob, who gave us the well and drank from it himself, as did also his sons and his flocks and herds?"

Jesus answered, "Everyone who drinks this water will be thirsty again, but whoever drinks the water I give him will never thirst. Indeed, the water I give him will become in him a spring of water welling up to eternal life."

The woman said to him, "Sir, give me this water so that I won't get thirsty and have to keep coming her to draw water."

He told her, "Go, call your husband and come back."

"I have no husband," she replied.

Jesus said to her, "You are right when you say you have no husband. The fact is, you have had five husbands, and the man you now have is not your husband. What you have just said is quite true."

"Sir," the woman said, "I can see that you are a prophet. Our fathers worshipped on this mountain, but you Jews claim that the place we must worship is in Jerusalem."

Jesus declared, "Believe me, woman, a time is coming when you will worship the Father neither on this mountain nor in Jerusalem. You Samaritans worship what you do not know. We worship what we do know, for salvation is coming from the Jews. God is spirit, and his worshipers must worship in sprit and in truth."

The woman said, "I know that Messiah (called Christ) is coming. When he comes, he will explain everything to us."

Then Jesus declared, "I who speak to you am he."

Interpretation

Mary Ann Getty-Sullivan in *Women in the New Testament* gives us a framework for viewing this verbal exchange. It was unusual in a number of ways. It was unusual for a woman to be alone by the well at noon – she would normally be with a group of women. It was unusual for a Jew to ask a Samaritan for a drink. As the conversation ensued, the subject moved from the physical to the spiritual.

In the conversation, this woman is faced with the decision to live in reality or illusion. She has been "called out" by Jesus speaking the truth of her life. Luckily no one has yet joined them. Can you imagine being in a public place, and approached by a man with whom you should not even converse, much less provide support? This woman attempted to create an illusion of her life in her confrontation and questioning of Jesus and he saw through her. Through the exchange, she saw through her own illusion of the Hebrew man. She had the vision to stay and talk with a man she saw as a prophet and to bring her kinsmen as well to hear him speak. She was instrumental in planting seeds for the future in her community.

Willow Bible Mother Meditation
Pharaoh's Daughter and the Woman of Samaria

You are seated in a space of darkness. It is midnight. Visualize an anchor of light coming from the top of your head down through your feet and hooking into the core of the earth. Breathe deeply sending energy down this cord and see it coming back up into your being.

You are standing at the entrance to a fun zone in a carnival and you are accompanied by two women. Pharaoh's Daughter is tall and stately with black hair in plaits down her back. A Woman of Samaria is clothed in a blue shift and her curly auburn hair frames her face. Both women give you a wink and ask, "Are you ready?"

They walk with you to the house of mirrors and encourage you to go in and face your illusions. As you enter, pay attention to the images you find inside. What illusions are you maintaining in your life? Which ones are you ready to shatter and move into reality? Once you recognize those illusions, Pharaoh's Daughter hands you a hammer to use to shatter the mirrors.

On the other side, you find open ground in furrows, ready for planting. The seeds are in your inner pocket. Walk over when you're ready and plant your seeds. The Woman of Samaria will greet you and give you a watering can to water each of your seeds. Take your time. Be persistent in your planting and your care. Once you feel complete, join the two women and they will bring you back to your room.

Pharaoh's Daughter and the Woman of Samaria Worksheet

1. Did you recognize these women when you met them? Who did they resemble?

2. How did it feel to enter the hall of mirrors?

3. What illusions did you face?

4. Which seeds did you cultivate?

Tina Carey

Images of Bible Mothers
Pharaoh's Daughter and the Woman of Samaria

Key Word Journal for Bible Mothers
Pharaoh's Daughter and the Woman of Samaria

Key Words of Empowerment

- Planting seeds
- Renewal, Nurturing
- Cultivation
- Expectation
- Perseverance, concentration
- Earth connection, grounding wisdom
- Illusion/reality

June 25th

HAWTHORN HUATHE

©1997 Katherine Torres, Ph. D., Transpersonal Development

Hawthorn Celtic Moon Mother

She signifies the empowerment of the coming of summer and the delight in opportunities to be playful. Her ribbons of green and yellow represent the intuitive (green) and logical (yellow) mind. The stones across her eyebrow remind you to stay alert and bring the two qualities of your mind into union. The flowers of orange and white are to remind you to beautify your life and be playful.

Time of Year

Hawthorn reflects the power of the sun in Gemini.

Key Words of Empowerment

- Clear communication
- Discernment
- Choices
- Clarity of consciousness
- Playfulness
- Retrieving knowledge in both the physical and spiritual worlds

Personal Inspiration

Clear Communication—In 2003, I began a new assignment for one of my clients in Pennsylvania. Just before I came on board there had been an accident – a chemical release into the atmosphere. Luckily no one was hurt, but I was able to discern a flaw in one of the corporate processes that allowed this to happen. I chose to speak up and ensure that "the powers that be" were aware of the potential for harm and a possible solution to the issue.

Discernment—During the Hawthorn Moon time, I began the High Priestess level for the *Daughters of the Moon* working earnestly on the project of writing this book. My discernment was clarity in understanding of the importance of these decisions and the actions I took to make them a reality.

Playfulness/Clear Communication—I had the honor of hosting an event for my idol, folksinger Judy Collins. It was a dream come true for me to spend the day with her. What a pleasure for me! I gained tremendous knowledge and insight from the experience that was reflected in a presentation I made at the event. The following day a gentleman who had attended the event told me that my clear communication had touched his heart and he wanted to give something back to me--an 8 X 10 picture of me with Judy Collins. What a treasure!

Choices—It was during the time of Hawthorn (in fact the same evening as the Judy Collins event) that I was recognized by the Order of St. Stanislas for support I had provided for their charitable organization. I was presented with the Silver Medal of Merit. My choice to support this organization had resulted in tremendous recognition.

Bible Mothers for Hawthorn Celtic Moon

Old Testament – Queen Vashti

New Testament – Lydia

Hawthorn Bible Mother—Old Testament
Queen Vashti

Scripture: Esther 1:9-12

Queen Vashti also gave a banquet for the women in the royal palace of King Xerses. On the seventh day, when King Xerses was in high spirits from wine, he commanded the seven eunuchs who served him . . . to bring before him Queen Vashti, wearing her royal crown, in order to display her beauty to the people and nobles, for she was lovely to look at. But when the attendants delivered the king's command, Queen Vashti refused to come. Then the king became furious and burned with anger.

Interpretation

Queen Vashti was known to be one of the most beautiful women in King Xerses' realm. She was a Persian Princess by birth, with power and value of her own. In this story, her husband, King Xerxes, invited many nobles for a week long celebration. Queen Vashti created the hospitality, beauty and **playful** environment for a successful gathering. The related scripture speaks of lavish gardens within the court in addition to the surroundings and welcome nature of the environment.

Vashti's challenge and **choice** occurs seven days into the celebration. Her husband and friends had been drinking steadily and his demands surely came from a place of drunkenness when he requested that she appear before all the guests to simply "show her beauty." When giving this command, Xerses knew that in Vashti's home culture, this would be a gross insult. In fact, this was an inappropriate request. Vashti's **choice** was to deny her husband's request, as she believed conscience and dignity were higher ideals than obedience.

Herbert Lockyear in his book, *Women of the Bible*, notes that Vashti chose to sacrifice a kingdom rather than cater to the vanity and sensuality of her husband and friends. She accepted dismissal and disgrace rather than lower her standards of modesty exhibiting **clarity of consciousness** in her actions. As Lockyear notes, "The only true ruler in that drunken court was the woman who refused to exhibit herself, even at the king's command."

Vashti represents the face of the Divine Feminine in this story and resonates with the message and energy of Celtic Moon Mother Hawthorn. She exhibits clear capacity for hospitality, warmth and **playfulness** for seven straight days. Vashti exhibits the ability to be the penultimate hostess through creating delight for a large group of the nobility of her time. She is faced in the midst of her hospitality with an ultimate choice between belittling herself in front of this large group of men, or standing her ground and risking her throne.

Celtic Moon Mother Hawthorn represents "Heart Integrity" and Queen Vashti looked to her own heart integrity when she refused her husband's command. She stood firm in her role as Queen and did not stoop to what she considered an inappropriate request. Her **clarity of choice** when asked to belittle herself resulted in a personal sacrifice.

Hawthorn Bible Mother—New Testament
Lydia

Scripture: Acts 16:12-15

On the Sabbath we went outside the city gates to the river, where we expected to find a place of prayer. We sat down and began to speak to the women who had gathered there. One of those listening was a woman named Lydia, a dealer in purple cloth from the city of Thyatira, who was a worshiper of God. The Lord opened her heart to respond to Paul's message. When she and the members of her household were baptized, she invited us to her home. "If you consider me a believer in the Lord," she said, "come and stay at my house." And she persuaded us.

Interpretation

Lydia is described as "the woman who was diligent in business." In Nell Mahoney's book, *From Mary to Lydia – Letting the New Testament Women Speak to Us*, it states that, "Her personal appearance turned heads as she walked down the streets of Philippi. She was a tall, stately woman with dark hair and 'laughing eyes.' In addition, she always wore purple. It was extremely becoming on her and it was also good for business, for she was a dealer in purple cloth."

Lydia was a liberated woman who owned and successfully operated her own business. Lydia was a woman of vision, enthusiasm, hospitality, focus and mental acumen. She also was a seeker for the spiritual side of life and this search brought her to listen to Paul and Silas that day by the side of the river. Herbert Lockyear notes that she hungered for a deeper spiritual experience and her mind opened as she listened to the teachings of Paul sharing the vision and leadership of the life of Jesus.

Lydia was a woman with **clarity of consciousness** and was driven to **retrieve knowledge** in both the physical world through her business and the spiritual world through her work with Paul and Silas.

Lydia's hospitality is shown through her welcoming of Paul and Silas into her home. She also becomes the hostess for the first Christian church in her city welcoming converts into her own home. As noted by Mary Ann Getty-Sullivan in *Women in the New Testament*, Lydia welcomed them even as they were released from jail. She and all the members of her household were baptized by Paul and Silas as well.

Lydia embodies many elements of Celtic Moon Mother Hawthorn. Both are decisive in their actions. Lydia was moved by the message of Jesus as told by Paul and welcomed that love into her heart. She immediately invited Paul and Silas to her home and became that "base of operations" for Phillipi. I can imagine the dexterity it took for Lydia to be prepared for the early church members to come into her home at a moment's notice. Sometimes they came and displayed joy in their work, and other times they came straight to her home from jail. Lydia created a safe place full of joy. She searched for knowledge, and was always willing to step forward into the role of leader as well as hostess. She is a multi-faceted woman who was a role model in her time for growth and expansion.

Hawthorn Bible Mother Meditation
Queen Vashti and Lydia

You are seated in a well-lit warm space. It is early morning. Visualize an anchor of light coming from the top of your head down through your feet and hooking into the core of the earth. Breathe deeply sending energy down this cord and see it coming back up into your being.

Visualize two women approaching you. On the left you see a woman in the ultimate regalia of a queen. She is in a long white dress with a purple robe that is clasped with a gold closure. On her head is a crown of silver and light filigree. She carries flowers for you that are colorful and fragrant. Next to her is a tall woman dressed in purple. Her head is covered with a beautiful scarf of various shades of purple. Her gift is also in her hands. It is a map of your upcoming journey.

Both women come to you smiling and greet you as one of their own. Vashti speaks first. She invites you to walk with them and experience the joy and responsibility of leadership. Lydia takes your hand as the three of you enter a new space. You walk through lush, fragrant gardens blazing with color.

You can feel the energy of the plants that grow there. With Vashti and Lydia at your side, you enter into a large courtyard filled with people. Vashti introduces you as the hostess for the upcoming gathering. Lydia acknowledges your planning and the beauty of the event. You see the ensuing gathering in the form of a fast forward movie and recognize your partnership in its success. You return to your room with Vashti and Lydia at either side. They leave you with their blessing as you carry their gifts with you.

Queen Vashti and Lydia Worksheet

1. *As you think back on your journey with Vashti and Lydia, what did they look like? What image do you have of them?*

2. *How did you feel when you realized you are the one responsible for the event you saw?*

3. *How do you respond to leadership roles in your everyday life?*

4. *What advice do Vashti and Lydia have for you?*

Tina Carey

Images of Bible Mothers

Queen Vashti and Lydia

Key Word Journal for Bible Mothers
Queen Vashti and Lydia

Key Words of Empowerment

- Clear communication
- Discernment
- Choices
- Clarity of consciousness
- Playfulness
- Retrieving knowledge in both the physical and spiritual worlds

OAK   DUIR

©1997 Katherine Torres, Ph. D., Transpersonal Development

Oak Celtic Moon Mother

She represents strength and empowerment. Her glow is that of balance: masculine (power of the sun) and feminine (soft glow of the moon). Her copper feathers represent the softness through balance and connection with spirit. The acorns represent fertility, virility, creativity and abundance; again balance of masculine and feminine. The mistletoe is the sacred plant of the Druidess that creates healing on all levels. It is also symbolic of ritual and sacred ceremonies.

Time of Year

Oak reflects the power of the sun in Cancer. It honors the celebration of Summer Soltice.

Key Words of Empowerment

- Protector
- Creator, Pregnancy
- Family, Home
- Ancestry
- Teacher, Healer
- Humanitarian
- Leader
- Service oriented

Personal Inspiration

Family/Home—Oak is the time of year where the energy of "The Great Mother" is apparent. In 2002, my mother energy came into place with my boys' graduation from high school. I also found myself in many family gatherings during Oak. My kids surprised me by redecorating my living room while I was on a European trip during this cycle of Oak.

Service Oriented—In 2005, I enjoyed several service-oriented events:

- I created the Merchant Angel Network partnering with a number of local merchants to support local charities. Eleven businesswomen came together each quarter to donate 5% of our sales one Thursday per month for a local charity.
- I met Jana Halverson who is a young woman driven to serve others in many charitable ways. With Jana, our merchant area was able to help the victims of Hurricane Katrina in Los Angeles at the Dream Center. Jana became our driver who picked up food from various markets, collected the money gathered by the

merchants and delivered new toys for the children affected by this tragedy.

- My friend, Priscilla Dewey, fell and broke her hip. I found myself in the role of healer, advocate and supporter during her time of recuperation. This support ranged from actually providing hands-on healing in the hospital, to being the link back to her family during her hospital stay.

Bible Mothers for Oak Celtic Moon Mother

Old Testament – Sarah

New Testament – Elizabeth

Oak Bible Mother—Old Testament
Sarah

Scripture: Genesis 17:15-17, 18:10-14

God also said to Abraham, "As for Sarai, your wife, you are no longer to call her Sarai; her name will be Sarah. I will bless her and will surely give you a son by her. I will bless her so that she will be the mother of nations; kings of peoples will come from her."

Abraham fell facedown; he laughed and said to himself, Will a son be born to a man a hundred years old? Will Sarah bear a child at the age of ninety?

Then the Lord said, "I will surely return to you about this time next year and Sarah, your wife will have a son." Now Sarah was listening at the entrance to the tent, which was behind him. Abraham and Sarah were already old and well advanced in years, and Sarah was past the age of child bearing. So Sarah laughed to herself as she thought, "After I am worn out and my master is old, will I now have this pleasure?"

Then the Lord said to Abraham, "Why did Sarah laugh and say, "Will I really have a child, now that I am old?" "Is anything too hard for the Lord? I will return to you at the appointed time next year and Sarah will have a son."

Interpretation

For the Old Testament woman, I chose Sarah. Sarah has a "sacramental" name given by God/Goddess in association with a promise. It is the symbol of a covenant between Sarah and the Divine.

Sarah was a beautiful woman and grew more beautiful with age. As noted by Herbert Lockyear in *Women of the Bible*, even at 90 years old, she was so beautiful that Abraham was afraid that kings would fall in love with her – and two did! She is considered one of most beautiful women who ever lived.

In the story we discover a very powerful woman. As noted by Irene Nowell in

Women of the Old Testament, all her adult life, Sarah taught the other women about God. She was recognized as a **leader** by her husband, as he would set her tent up first. In a nomadic tribe, this was a certain sign of respect and leadership within the tribe.

When Sarah overheard Abraham being told of her impending pregnancy, she laughed. Her laughter exposed her to Abraham, but he did not scorn her – in fact, he had laughed himself when God first told him of the impending birth.

In the message of the Lord, Sarah's pregnancy is referred to as a "rebirth of season" – the birth of a nation. Sarah was considered the Mother of a Nation.

While it sounds impossible, when Sarah was 90 years old, she gave birth to a child and nurtured that child to adulthood.

Oak Bible Mother—New Testament

Elizabeth

Scripture: Luke 1:11-13, 18-24, 39-45

Then an angel of the Lord appeared to him, standing at the right side of the altar of incense. When Zecharaia saw him, he was startled and was gripped with fear. But the angel said to him: "Do not be afraid, Zecharaiah; your prayer has been heard. Your wife Elizabeth will bear you a son, and you are to give him the name of John."

Zecharaiah asked the angel, "How can I be sure of this? I am an old man and my wife is well along in years." The angel answered, "I am Gabriel. I stand in the presence of God, and I have been sent to speak to you and to tell you this good news. And now you will be silent and not able to speak until the day this happens, because you did not believe my words, which will come true at their proper time."

Meanwhile, the people were waiting for Zecharaiah and wondering why he stayed so long in the temple. When he came out, he could not speak to them. They realized he had seen a vision in the temple, for he kept making signs to them, but remained unable to speak. When his time of service was completed, he returned home. After this, his wife, Elizabeth become pregnant and for five months remained in seclusion.

At that time Mary got ready and hurried to a town in the hill country of Judea, where she entered Zecharaiah's home and greeted Elizabeth. When Elizabeth heard Mary's greeting, the baby leaped in her womb, and Elizabeth was filled with the Holy Spirit. In a loud voice she exclaimed, "Blessed are you among women, and blessed is the child you will bear! But why am I so favored, that the mother of the Lord should come to me? As soon as the sound of your greeting reached my ears, the baby in my womb leaped for joy. Blessed is she who has believed that what the Lord has said to her will be accomplished!"

Interpretation

I decided that Mother Mary is a well known figure to everyone and considered a classic model of the Divine mother. So, I chose to honor the gifts of a lesser known Bible mother, Elizabeth.

Elizabeth, like Sarah, bore a child in her old age. I see her as a woman well into her Wyse Woman time, carrying both male and female strengths of character. Elizabeth was a priestly wife and a teacher and "priest" herself within the temple. As described by Herbert Lockyear in *Women of the Bible*, she was a priestly woman of "unusual piety, strong faith and spiritual gifts." She served in the temple next to her husband carrying stature and privilege.

Her husband was struck dumb during her **pregnancy** in response to the miracle of conception. This was in response to his doubt of the potential miracle. On the other hand as noted by Mary Ann Getty-Sullivan in *Women of the New Testament*, Elizabeth never faltered in her faith, nor did she doubt the power of God's miracle. During her pregnancy, Elizabeth became a voice for her husband. She was the living example of the **miracle of creation** and lived that belief.

Her intuition was extremely strong. When Mary came to visit her, Elizabeth recognized not only Mary's pregnant state, but with the child she carried, she recognized the Avatar to come in Jesus. As noted in Lockyear, it was Elizabeth's spirit filled greeting that inspired Mary to reply in song of "The Magnificat."

Oak Bible Mother Meditation
Sarah and Elizabeth

You are seated in a softly lit room of mid-morning light. Visualize an anchor of light coming from the top of your head down through your feet and hooking into the core of the earth. Breathe deeply sending energy down this cord and see it coming back up into your being.

You find yourself in a space of peaceful openness. You are greeted by two grandmotherly women. They come to you in tandem; each one is carrying energy of light, knowledge and wisdom. On the left you see a woman of graying hair and great beauty, her blue eyes shine as she greets you. On your right side, you see a tall woman with reddish hair. Her green eyes welcome you to her home. They lead you into a cozy room. They seat you in front of a cheery fire and share stories. They are present to care for you and give you the opportunity to share secrets with them. They hold all of your confidences in great respect and add their nurturing energy to your dreams. You doze easily in your seat and allow them to care for you.

When you awake, they bring you a gift of a cloth, which you can use in your own space, or even wrap yourself in when in need of comfort. They bless you and send you home.

Sarah and Elizabeth Worksheet

1. When you saw Sarah and Elizabeth who did they resemble? Anyone you recognized?

2. What stories did they share with you?

3. What dreams did you share with them?

4. How are you "pregnant with possibilities?"

Tina Carey

Images of Bible Mothers
Sarah and Elizabeth

Key Word Journal for Bible Mothers
Sarah and Elizabeth

Key Words of Empowerment

- Protector
- Creator, Pregnancy
- Family, Home
- Ancestry
- Teacher, Healer
- Humanitarian
- Leader
- Service oriented

Holly Celtic Moon Mother

She reflects an expression of joy, purpose, strength and confidence. The snake around her eyes reveals the spiritual fire coiled at the base of the spine that has risen and conscious awareness of one's True Self/Divine Self is known. The infinity sign of the snake figure shows the power of balance, the union of the Divine, and the ability to maintain a central state of consciousness while living in the world of polarities. Peacock feathers around the face provide the power of "seeing" all around (inside and out, above and below); being in a state of conscious awareness. There is the strength of masculine consciousness through the essence of the feminine.

Time of Year

Holly reflects the power of the sun in Leo. It also reveals the Celebration of Lammas (first harvest of the year).

Key Words of Empowerment

- Joy
- Purpose
- Strength
- Confidence
- Recognition
- Proud
- Bold
- Optimism
- Courage

Personal Inspiration

Purpose/Courage—I began my journey with the Celtic Moon Mothers and entered the first level of the *Daughters of the Moon* in July – the time of Holly. As I came into the time of Holly, I had some enlightening realizations:

- I was responsible for many people my entire life – starting in my childhood.
- My married name, "Carey," set out the energy for me to "carry" others and that's what I did in my life.
- I was very good at carrying more than my part of a relationship.

Strength/Courage—In the Holly time of 2001, I began to step away from relationships that were out of balance. I set different boundaries for myself (you'll see examples of this also reflected in Esther's story with my children, the men in my life and even my relationship with my clients).

Joy/Purpose/Recognition—It was during the time of Holly that I began to work with representatives for folk singer, Judy Collins who made an appearance at my bookstore giving me a new and different kind of attention. I found a new joy and purpose in the time of Holly recognizing the powerful woman living inside me and allowing her to be publicly recognized as well.

Bible Mothers for Holly Celtic Moon Mother

Old Testament – Queen Esther

New Testament – Mary Magdalene

Old Testament Holly Bible Mother
Queen Esther

Scripture: Esther 2:17-18, 21-23, 3:1-6, 7:1-10

Now the king was attracted to Esther more than to any of the other women, and she won his favor and approval more than any of the other virgins. So he set a royal crown on her head and made her queen instead of Vashti. And the king gave a great banquet, Esther's banquet, for all his nobles and officials. He proclaimed a holiday throughout the provinces and distributed gifts with royal liberality.

During the time Mordecai was sitting at the king's gate, Bigthana and Teresh, two of the king's officers who guarded the doorway, became angry and conspired to assassinate King Xerses. But Mordecai found out about the plot and told Queen Esther, who in turn reported it to the king, giving credit to Mordecai. And when the report was investigated and found to be true, the two officials were hanged on the gallows.

After these events, King Xerses honored Haman, son of Hammedatha, the Agagite, elevating him and giving him a seat of honor higher than that of all the other nobles. All the royal officials at the king's gate knelt down and paid honor to Haman, for the king had commanded this concerning him. But Modecai would not kneel down or pay him honor.

Then the royal officials at the king's gate asked Mordecai, "Why do you disobey the king's command?" Day after day they spoke to him but he refused to comply. Therefore they told Haman about it to see whether Mordecai's behavior would be tolerated, for he had told them he was a Jew.

When Haman saw that Mordecai would not kneel down or pay him honor, he was enraged. Yet having learned who Mordecai's people were, he scorned the idea of killing only Mordecai. Instead Haman looked for a way to destroy all Mordecai's people, the Jews, throughout the whole kingdom of Xerses.

So the king and Haman went to dine with Queen Esther, and as they were drinking wine on that second day, the king again asked, "Queen Esther, what is your petition? It will be given to you. What is your request? Even up to half the kingdom, it will be granted."

Then Queen Esther answered, "If I have found favor with you, O king, and if it pleases your majesty, grant me my life – this is my petition. And spare my people – this is my request. For I and my people have been sold for destruction and slaughter and annihilation. If we had merely been sold as male and female slaves, I would have kept quiet, because no such distress would justify disturbing the king."

King Xerses asked Queen Esther, "Who is he? Where is the man who has dared to do such a thing?"

Esther said, "The adversary and enemy is this vile Haman."

Then Haman was terrified before the king and queen. The king got up in a rage, left his wine and went out into the palace garden. But Haman, realizing that the king had already decided his fate, stayed behind to beg Queen Esther for his life.

Just as the king returned from the palace garden to the banquet hall, Haman was falling on the couch where Esther was reclining.

The king exclaimed, "Will he even molest the queen while she is with me in the house?"

As soon as the word left the king's mouth, they covered Haman's face. Then Harbona, one of the eunuchs attending the king, said, "A gallows seventy-five feet high stands by Haman's house. He had it made for Mordecai, who spoke up to help the king."

The king said, "Hang him on it!" So they hanged Hamon on the gallows he had prepared for Mordecai. Then the king's fury subsided.

Interpretation

Esther was selected to be Queen by King Xerses after he sent Queen Vashti out for refusing to appear in front of his guests. Esther was selected from all the women in the kingdom because she was the most beautiful. Additionally as noted by Lockyer in *The Women of the Bible* through her beauty there shone a radiance of personality and character which enhanced her beauty and gave distinction in the eyes of the King.

She also hid the fact that she was a Jew. She stood up and took her place as queen. When a plot was hatched to kill all of the Jews, she had the **strength, courage** and ingenuity to bring the truth to the king and to avoid disaster for her people. All of these attributes are elements of the Celtic Moon Mother Holly and her time of the year in the summer of the sign Leo. She wore the cloak of leadership well in her role as Queen. She was willing to stand out, to speak up and to embody truth in her life. She became the center of attention and in doing so, saved her people.

This reminded me of the Cinderella story. She was sought out and found to be the most beautiful and eventually also found to be the wisest. As noted by Irene Nowell in *Women in the Old Testament*, Esther is a beautiful young woman, initially passive until the crisis of the potential destruction of her people creates the opportunity for her to step into her full potential with confidence.

The man who hatched the plot to have the Jews killed was Haman, one of the King's advisors. In *The Midrash*, the story is flushed out even further:

"The Archangel Michael was the defense attorney for the Jewish people before God, the judge of all. Haman, as prosecutor, leveled charge after charge against the Jews. Michael answered every one of these charges. In the summation, Michael contended that Jews were guilty of refusing to bow to idols or shed blood. Their only crime had been keeping God's laws. Hearing this, the one who judges all hearts reaffirmed the divine covenant never to forsake the Jewish people. (Esther Rabbah 7.12)

Holly Bible Mother—New Testament
Mary Magdalene

Scripture: John 20:10-18

Then the disciples went back to their homes, but Mary stood outside the tomb crying. As she wept, she bent over to look into the tomb and saw two angels in white, seated where Jesus' body had been, one at the head and the other at the foot. They asked her, "Woman, why are you crying?"

"They have taken my Lord away," she said, "and I don't know where they have put him."

At this, she turned around and saw Jesus standing there, but she did not realize that it was Jesus. "Woman," he said, "why are you crying? Who is it you are looking for?"

Thinking he was the gardener, she said, "Sir, if you have carried him away. Tell me where you have put him, and I will get him."

Jesus said to her, "Mary."

She turned toward him and cried out in Aramaic, "Rabboni!" (which means Teacher).

Jesus said, "Do not hold on to me, for I have not yet returned to the Father. Go instead to my brothers and tell them, 'I am returning to my Father, to my God and to your God.'"

Mary Magdalene went to the disciples with the news: "I have seen the Lord!" And she told them that he had said these things to her.

Interpretation

In recent times, Mary Magdalene has become more significant than we were taught in the past. The essence of the Holly vibration is attention—being in the center of attention. From our first experience of Mary Magdalene with Jesus, she is the center of attention. The gospel speaks of her being healed by Jesus curing her of possession by demons (7 in fact). She certainly was the center of attention for that to happen – and publicly.

There has been much inference of Mary's character in the history of the church, but as noted by Herbert Lockyer in *The Women of the Bible*, there is no evidence that she was a prostitute or a "fallen woman." As he states, she is one of the most faithful and beautiful characters of the Bible.

Mary Magdalene had a place of power and **recognition** at the miracle of the Resurrection. Mary Magdalene was the one at the tomb and Jesus called to her directly. As is noted by Mary Ann Getty-Sullivan, Mary Magdalene is referenced in all four Gospels as a witness to the crucifixion and the resurrection.

Mary was, in my estimation, a fun-loving person. She was a leader among the disciples, one who spoke her mind with dignity and was respected by Jesus and his followers. In fact, it was she who announced to the other disciples that "I have seen the Lord" and she was believed. The men followed her to the tomb.

I can visualize Mary with Jesus and the apostles reminding them not to take themselves too seriously and to recognize the beauty in each day as they came to teach and preach. She knew that the underlying message of love was the key message and kept them focused on the message as well as the messenger.

She brought comfort to Jesus, calming him in times of crisis and shielding him by becoming the focus when necessary. She used all of her talents to be his partner in ministry and carry on in his absence. Her womanhood was recognized as **strength** and a value to the disciples.

In her Holly way, she was beautiful, and a star. She was recognized by all as Jesus' partner and blessed for her beauty, talents and willingness to share her knowledge and peace with others. She helped to create community, to knit the energy of family between the disciples as they trekked both with Jesus and after his passing.

She carried the seeds of the key message of the Love of the Divine and worked to bring that message into the light for all people, men and women alike. She reflected Jesus' teachings to the world in her own way.

Holly Bible Mother Meditation
Queen Esther and Mary Magdalene

You are seated in a warm, dim space of late afternoon light. Visualize an anchor of light coming from the top of your head down through your feet and hooking into the core of the earth. Breathe deeply sending energy down this cord and see it coming back up into your being.

As you relax, you are greeted by two gorgeous women. On your left is a Queen, a woman of great beauty and charm. She stands out in her finery of turquoise robes and silver jewelry. She brings the gift of a mirror. Esther encourages you to look at your reflection in the world and to recognize your own power. Within the mirror is reflected the essence of your own royalty and your ability to become visible in your world.

On your right is a woman of great courage and strength. Her dress is a deep blue color and sets off the red fire in her hair. Mary Magdalene speaks to you of courage and willingness to step up and speak your truth. She brings you a peacock feather and speaks of ensuring your inner "plumage" is in order.

They take you to a clear pond. You look into the pond at your reflection and are gifted with a personal movie of your place in the world – a vision of your own strength and potential. You hear your words of empowerment that are meant to be shared with others and see yourself illuminated and filled with the attention you deserve. Enjoy your time with these women. When you see the vision begin to fade, they will escort you back to your space and leave you with their blessing.

Queen Esther and Mary Magdalene Worksheet

1. *When you saw Queen Esther and Mary Magdalene, did you recognize them? Do they resemble anyone you know? If so, whom?*

2. *When you looked at your reflection, what did you see?*

3. *What were the symbols you saw of your strength and potential?*

4. *How did you respond to your own royalty?*

Images of Bible Mothers
Queen Esther and Mary Magdalene

Key Word Journal for Bible Mothers
Queen Esther and Mary Magdalene

Key Words of Empowerment

- Joy
- Purpose
- Strength
- Confidence
- Recognition
- Proud
- Bold
- Optimism
- Courage

Hazel Celtic Moon Mother

Her salmon-colored face provides an expression of wisdom and faith, ease and peace. Her green eyes reveal the nurturing and creative power within. Green, associated with the Great Fertile Mother, is a reminder that the eyes of the Great Mother lovingly looks upon you to nurture and care for you. The Dragon reveals all knowledge consciously acknowledged and the spiritual fire coiled at the base of the spine has truly risen. The salmon and the hazel nut depict the power of wisdom assimilated, seen and used.

Time of Year

Hazel reflects the power of the sun in Virgo. The honoring of summer to fall is seen by the transforming beauty of plants, the animals changing actions and the attitudes of people.

Key Words of Empowerment

- Absolute Faith
- Knowing
- Wisdom
- Trust
- No doubts
- No urgency

Personal Inspiration

Absolute Faith—For me, Hazel is the time of the year when I find myself walking in faith. Much of the work I do is internal – on the inner planes in meditation. As I do the internal work, changes happen in the external world. For example, it was during the time of Hazel I first heard of a wonderful woman named Priscilla Dewey.

I was led to Priscilla for a specific purpose. She has an instrument called a biometer that measures a person's awareness – one's soul evolution. The decision to work with Priscilla has been one that has changed many elements in my life. This instrument combined with her coaching helped me to understand the potential I brought into this lifetime. Because of the profound impact her work had on me, I took my children to Priscilla and have referred many friends and acquaintances.

Wisdom/Trust—I go to Maui for spiritual renewal and many times I'm there during this time of year. I walk a path of faith and am gifted with many signs of support. In 2005 during the time of Hazel, I experienced:

- Rainbows for breakfast

- Seeing a rainbow of moonlight encircling Molokai
- Inspiration for an intention statement that led to writing this book.

Bible Mothers for Hazel Celtic Moon Mother

Old Testament – Ruth

New Testament – Mary the mother of Jesus

Hazel Bible Mother—Old Testament
Ruth

Scripture: Ruth 1:3-17, 2:11-12

Now Elimelech, Naomi's husband, died, and she was left with her two sons. They married Moabite women, one named Orpah and the other, Ruth. After they had lived there about ten years, both Mahlon and Kilion also died, and Naomi was left without her two sons and her husband.

When she heard in Moab that the Lord had come to the aid of his people by providing food for them, Naomi and her daughters-in-law prepared to return home from there. With her two daughters-in-law she left the place where she had been living and set out on the road that would take them back to the land of Judah.

Then Naomi said to her two daughters-in-law, "Go back, each of you, to your mother's home. May the Lord show kindness to you, as you have shown to your dead and to me. May the Lord grant that each of you will find rest in the home of another husband."

Then she kissed them and they wept aloud and said to her, "We will go back with you to your people."

But Naomi said, "Return home, my daughters. Why would you come with me? Am I going to have any more sons who could become your husbands? Return home, my daughters; I am too old to have another husband…"

And they wept again. Then Orpah kissed her mother-in-law good-by, but Ruth clung to her.

"Look," said Naomi, "your sister-in-law is going back to her people and her gods. Go back with her."

But Ruth replied, "Don't urge me to leave you or to turn back from you. Where you go I will go, and where you stay, I will stay. Your people will be my people and your God my God. Where you die, I will die, and there I will be buried. May the Lord deal with me, be it ever so severely, if anything but death separates you and me."

Boaz replied, "I've been told all about what you have done for your mother-in-law since the death of your husband – how you left your father and mother and your homeland and came to live with a people you did not know before. May the Lord repay you for what you have done. May you be richly rewarded by the Lord, the God of Israel, under whose wings, you have dome to take refuge."

Interpretation

In the Old Testament, the story of Ruth is a story of Faith. Ruth chose to remain with Naomi, her mother-in-law, even though it meant traveling to a new land. The famous words of "whither thou goest, I will go; whither thou lodgest, I will lodge; thy people shall be my people, and thy God my God" are Ruth's. It requires true fearlessness and **absolute faith** to follow another into uncertainty.

Ruth and her sister-in-law Orpah had been widowed, as had their mother-in-law Naomi. As noted by Herbert Lockyer in *Women of the Bible,* Naomi, her husband and two sons had come to Moab to escape a famine in their home of Bethlehem. Both sons had married Moabite women (Ruth and Orpah). After ten years, both brothers had died leaving Ruth and Orpah childless. Their father had also died in Moab leaving all three women widows.

As noted by Irene Nowell in *Women in the Old Testament*, Ruth's future appeared to be hopeless. Israelites were forbidden to marry Moabites. Israelite men were encouraged to marry the widows in the family – there were no men left in Naomi's family. And still, Ruth stayed and trusted Naomi.

Once they reached Bethlehem, Ruth continued to listen to Naomi and through her advice, Ruth found her new husband, Boaz. Ruth **trusts** Naomi and stands in her own integrity.

Ruth's story is one of the women who had to stand alone due to the loss of her husband. As noted by Helen Bruch Pearson in her book, *Mother Roots*, Ruth's story is about inclusion – about **faith** that binds family in spite of differences in ethnicities and religion. Her response was serenity and a deep knowing that all would be all right. She had found in her mother-in-law, Naomi, a home for her heart.

Hazel Bible Mother—New Testament
Mary, Mother of Jesus

Scripture: Luke 1:26-38, 2:16-20, John 19:25-27

In the sixth month, God sent the angel Gabriel to Nazareth, a town in Galilee, to a virgin pledged to be married to a man named Joseph, a descendant of David. The virgin's name was Mary. The angel went to her and said, "Greetings, you who are highly favored! The Lord is with you."

Mary was greatly troubled at his words and wondered what kind of greeting this might be. But the angel said to her, "Do not be afraid, Mary, you have found favor with God. You will be with child and give birth to a son, and you are to give him the name Jesus. He will be great and will be called the Son of the Most High. The Lord God will give him the throne of his father David, and he will reign over the house of Jacob forever; his kingdom will never end."

"How will this be," Mary asked the angel, "since I am a virgin?"

The angel answered, "The Holy Spirit will come upon you, and the power of the Most High will overshadow you. So the holy one to be born will be called the Son of God. Even Elizabeth your relative is going to have a child in her old age, and she who was said to be barren is in her sixth month. For nothing is impossible with God."

"I am the Lord's servant," Mary answered. "May it be to me as you have said." Then the angel left her.

So they hurried off and found Mary and Joseph, and the baby, who was lying in the manger. When they had seen him, they spread the word concerning what had been told them about this child, and all who heard it were amazed at what the shepherds said to them. But Mary treasured up all these things and pondered them in her heart. The shepherds returned, glorifying and praising God for all the things they had heard and seen, which were just as they had been told.

Near the cross of Jesus stood his mother, his mother's sister, Mary the wife of

Clopas, and Mary Magdalene. When Jesus saw his mother there, and the disciple who he loved standing nearby, he said to his mother, "Dear woman, here is your son," and to the disciple, "Here is your mother." From that time on, this disciple took her into his home.

Interpretation

Mary was an example of faith from the early stories. As noted by Herbert Lockyer in *The Women of the Bible,* Mary first conceived Jesus in her heart by faith before she conceived in the womb. She first heard of her impending pregnancy from an angelic visitation. We see her as willing, if not ready – as described by Mary Ann Getty-Sullivan in *Women in the New Testament*. She responds with wonder, and believes.

As noted by Lockyer, Luke's gospel is one of a physician who provided Mary with the opportunity to speak intimately of her profound experience. It is her **faith**, and quiet spirit that we see through the narrative. Early in her life, we are told she observes the shepherds, the wise men, and the angels, and "ponders them in her heart."

We see glimpses of Mary's **faith** throughout the Gospel stories. Can you imagine the **faith** it took to allow your young son to disappear and then find him in the temple with the rabbis and scribes?

As noted by Mary Ann Getty-Sullivan, it was Mary who encouraged Jesus to perform his first miracle – the turning of water to wine. And this act became the first "sign" of his ministry. Mary had **faith** in her son, and instructed the servants to follow his instructions. We see her **faith** throughout his ministry.

Mary stayed present, even at the crucifixion. We see her standing, in her **faith**, holding the space as her son completes his destiny. She is with the other women at the tomb, initially preparing his body and then returning after the resurrection. She continued her son's work after his death, standing as the Mother of Faith for the disciples.

Hazel Bible Mother Meditation
Ruth and Mary, Mother of Jesus

You are seated in a comfortable, warm place of twilight. Visualize an anchor of light coming from the top of your head down through your feet and hooking into the core of the earth. Breathe deeply sending energy down this cord and see it coming back up into your being.

As you begin to relax you find yourself in the presence of two caring women. On your left is a woman who appears to have just come in from the fields. In her hands are sheaves of wheat which she hands to you. Her dark brown hair is braided down her back, and her dress is made of plain, rough cloth. Her feet are bare, and her green eyes carry a determined spark within. On your right, is a small woman dressed in pale blue. Her light brown hair is curly and light around her face and she brings a pink rose of love to you.

Ruth leads you to a table set for one. Mary sits next to you and Ruth brings you a hearty soup. You can feel the warmth of the liquid as you begin to eat. It warms you from the inside out. Ruth joins you, at your other side. These women sit silently as you slowly eat the soup. They offer you their comfort, presence and wisdom through their silent presence. When you finish, you sit with them, also in silence looking deep within for that power of faith. Looking into the eyes of each of the women, you can see the play of many emotions—joy, surprise, delight, anger, sadness, bewilderment, happiness—the entire rainbow of human emotion. You see, underneath it all, their ultimate and enduring faith.

Take comfort from them and allow that gift of faith to embrace and immerse you in its warmth. Once you feel the faith fully integrated into your soul, allow them to lead you home.

Ruth and Mary the Mother of Jesus Worksheet

1. How did Ruth and Mary appear to you? Did you recognize them? If so, who are they?

2. How did you respond to being cared for by these women?

3. How did it feel to be silent with these women? How did you respond?

4. How do you care for yourself?

Tina Carey

Images of Bible Mothers
Ruth and Mary, the Mother of Jesus

Key Word Journal for Bible Mothers
Ruth and Mary, the Mother of Jesus

Key Words of Empowerment

- Absolute Faith
- Knowing
- Wisdom
- Trust
- No doubts
- No urgency

GRAPE VINE ✦ MUIN

©1997 Katherine Torres, Ph. D., Transpersonal Development

Grape Vine Celtic Moon Mother

She reflects the expression of being filled with life, teaming with creative expression, accepting reward and experiencing abundance. Her grape colored eyes reveal the passion for higher, more spiritual goals. Grape Vine brings harvest, joy, dance and celebration to us.

Time of Year

Grape Vine reflects the sun in Virgo and Libra. At the proper moment, it heralds the Autumnal Equinox.

Key Words of Empowerment
- Celebration, Reward
- Harvesting, Dancing
- Passion for higher learning
- Spiritual goals
- Clear mind
- Light hearted

Personal Inspiration

Higher Learning—Looking back at the time of Grape Vine, I found many examples where I was working on the inner planes for higher learning. During the time of Grape Vine in 2001, our world experienced the terror of September 11th. My response to that tragic event was a time of internal exploration. I did a lot of meditation around healing and releasing anger, fear and pain. The drive for higher learning and spiritual goals are drives of Grape Vine.

Spiritual Goals—I entered the second level of the *Daughters of the Moon* program in the time of Grape Vine. Part of the process of entering the second or Priestess Level is to allow one of the Moon Mothers to come forward as your guide and mentor of a year of learning. My experience was quite delightful with the goddess Anu stepping forward (she is aligned with Hazel Moon Mother).

Celebration/Dancing—During the time of Grape Vine, I had a transition in one of my consulting assignments. My boss was moving out of the company. We held a delightful farewell party in Las Vegas that included dancing and partying until the wee hours of the morning.

Spiritual Goals/Celebration—In 2005, my Maui trip slid into the Grape Vine time as well as Hazel. When I returned home, I found that three of my photos had images of the celebration of spirit in them. Two of the photos are taken at sunset. They each have a beam of light entering the photo from a corner. The third is of me. I was in a restaurant (alone) for dinner. When the waiter brought my drink, he also brought me an orchid. I put the orchid behind my ear. The waiter commented that I looked beautiful and asked if he could he take my picture. The result is a picture that shows what appears to be a halo around my head. I found the photos to be energizing after a long flight and a confirmation of the celebration of life.

Bible Mothers for Grape Vine Celtic Moon Mother
Old Testament – Queen of Sheba

New Testament – Mary of Bethany

Grape Vine Bible Mother--Old Testament
Queen of Sheba

Scripture: I Kings 10:1-10, 13

When the Queen of Sheba heard about the fame of Solomon and his relation to the name of the Lord, she came to test him with hard questions. Arriving at Jerusalem with a very great caravan – with camels carrying spices, large quantities of gold, and precious stones – she came to Solomon and talked with him about all that she had on her mind. Solomon answered all her questions; nothing was too hard for the king to explain to her. When the queen of Sheba saw all the wisdom of Solomon and the palace he had built, the food on his table, the seating of his officials, the attending servants in their robes, his cupbearers, and the burnt offerings he made at the temple of the Lord, she was overwhelmed.

She said to the king, "The report I heard in my own country about your achievements and your wisdom is true. But I did not believe these things until I came and saw with my own eyes. Indeed, not even half was told me; in wisdom and wealth you have far exceeded the report I heard. How happy your officials, who continually stand before you and hear your wisdom! Praise be to the Lord your God, who had delighted in you and placed you on the throne of Israel. Because of the Lord's eternal love for Israel, he has made you king, to maintain justice and righteousness."

And she gave the king 120 talents of gold, large quantities of spices, and precious stones. Never again were so many spices brought in as those the queen of Sheba gave to King Solomon.

King Solomon gave the queen of Sheba all she desired and asked for, besides what he had given her out of his royal bounty. Then she left and returned with her retinue to her own country.

Interpretation

The Queen of Sheba is described as "the woman who loved wisdom" by Herbert Lockyer in *The Women of the Bible*. He notes that this is a woman who traveled a great distance to meet and visit with King Solomon. She came prepared to show respect and to celebrate the opportunity to learn from such a great Leader.

Irene Nowell states in *Women of the Old Testament* that she arrived with camels bearing spices and left with gifts from Solomon himself. I imagine her visit was a **celebration** of life and learning and harvested greatly for herself and her people. Being of royalty, her story still carries a **light-hearted energy** of willingness to venture out – of following her deep **intuition**. She was **clear-minded** in her intent and actions as she traveled and was also willing to learn new wisdom, and to share that harvest with her own people. She was rewarded and received great riches from Solomon himself due to her willingness to give and receive great learning.

Grape Vine Bible Mother—New Testament
Mary of Bethany - Sister of Martha and Lazarus

Scripture: Luke 10:38-41

As Jesus and his disciples were on their way, he came to a village where a woman named Martha opened her home to him. She had a sister called Mary, who sat at the Lord's feet listening to what he had said. But Martha was distracted by all the preparations that had to be made. She came to him and asked, "Lord, don't you care that my sister has left me to do the work by myself? Tell her to help me!"

"Martha, Martha," the Lord answered, "You are worried and upset about many things, but only one thing is needed. Mary has chosen what is better, and it will not be taken away from her."

Interpretation

In the story of Mary and Martha, Mary is the one willing to celebrate and enjoy the reward of having Jesus in her presence. Mary sees a different vision than Martha. Mary's focus is on the present moment – on enjoying the company of her teacher and her friend. Herbert Lockyer in *Women of the Bible* describes Mary of Bethany as an individualist. How many of us, as women, miss the opportunity of enjoyment, by not focusing on the "gift of the present moment" when it is presented to us?

Mary is open to that moment, and takes her place as she focuses her intention on receiving key information and enjoying being in the company of such a dear companion. Her commitment and willingness to listen to Jesus' teachings was an intuitive response to the present moment.

Nell W. Mahoney in "From Mary to Lydia" comments that Mary thinks in pictures and is very creative. She wants time to reflect, learn, think and enjoy. I see this Mary as light-hearted and yet clear-minded in recognizing her opportunity to see and learn from her Avatar.

Grape Vine Bible Mother Meditation
Queen of Sheba and Mary of Bethany,
Sister of Martha and Lazarus

You are seated in a cool, dim space. It is mid evening. Visualize an anchor of light coming from the top of your head down through your feet and hooking into the core of the earth. Breathe deeply sending energy down this cord and see it coming back up into your being.

As you enter your quiet space, you are joined by two women in varying shades of green. One is queenly in stature and her emerald green gown shimmers with golden highlights. Her auburn hair is elegantly fashioned and she hands you a dark green stone. Her counterpart is dressed in forest green, in beautiful, soft muslin and her dark blonde hair flows lightly around her face. She reaches out her hand to you and raises you to your feet. She hands you what looks like a diploma.

They are here to celebrate your spiritual graduation. With the Queen of Sheba and Mary of Bethany, you have been willing to listen, learn and quest for wisdom. They join you as you step up to your next level of learning. These women are dressed for celebration and lead you into a crowded room. On the dais are risers and on the risers are the ones who have traveled this path before you. There is one open space in the middle of the front row. You hear your name called. You are escorted to the risers by Mary of Bethany and the Queen of Sheba and take your rightful place. Feel the energy of those around you and allow the distinct essence of completeness to fill your soul.

Notice those in your presence and acknowledge the gifts they share with you. Notice the montage of all those souls and make a note in your unconscious so it becomes part of you. This is your graduating class and now you see the other alumni welcoming you. Allow yourself to step up, take your diploma and pocket your green stone. Return to your room alone.

Queen of Sheba and Mary of Bethany Worksheet

1. *When you saw the Queen of Sheba and Mary of Bethany, who did they resemble? Anyone you know?*

2. *How did it feel to "graduate" and receive your diploma?*

3. *Who was in your presence at the graduation?*

4. *What gifts did they share with you?*

Images of Bible Mothers
Queen of Sheba and Mary of Bethany

Key Word Journal for Bible Mothers
Queen of Sheba and Mary of Bethany

Key Words of Empowerment

- Celebration, Reward
- Harvesting, Dancing
- Passion for higher learning
- Spiritual goals
- Clear mind
- Light hearted

Ivy Celtic Moon Mother

She reflects mystery, stillness and intrigue. The twinkling jewels represent the stars in the night sky, the zodiac, planets and star paths of the Universe. The veil over her eyes holds a key to the truth that before you advance to the mysteries of the feminine; you need to learn about yourself through Still Movement. The overall veil represents a threshold—an entrance to the feminine mysteries and the secrets of women's spirituality. It is only lifted when one chooses to walk a sacred way. The cross signifies balance and the light rays are symbolic of the Holy Trinity—mother, daughter and Holy Spirit.

Time of Year

Ivy reflects her essence when the sun angles at Libra and ends at Scorpio

Key Words of Empowerment

- Mystery
- Stillness
- Intrigue
- Intuition
- Rhythm
- Balance

Personal Inspiration

Intuition—Ivy is a time for really listening to my inner voice and expanding my intuition. In looking back there have been many examples of Ivy's characteristics during this time. In 2001, my instructions for the *Daughters of the Moon* program were actually written on my birthday during the time of Ivy.

Balance—During the time of Ivy, I began working with the finance department of one of my clients. My project leader described my role with the CFO as his "balancing point" as we worked through this challenging time of change for the company.

Intrigue—It was during the time of Ivy that I went to court to gain guardianship/custody of my foster son. This is a young man who grew up around the corner from us. His mother passed away just before he and my sons entered high school. His mother's family did not want to take him in, so he came to live with us. I found out that his family was attempting to claim guardianship, when he actually lived with me. I was able to gain legal standing and began proceedings to become his guardian during Ivy.

Mystery/Stillness/Intuition—As I mentioned in the preface, it was during Ivy in 2005 that I wrote this book—a project that definitely tapped into the intuition and messages of Ivy's influence.

Mystery/Rhythm—In 2006, I took my trip to Maui in the time of Ivy. I experienced an earthquake while there. My initial plan was to be in Maui from October 8th to the 15th. Prior to departure, I changed my return date to the 20th to be available for a client. By changing my itinerary, I missed the chaos of traveling during the post-earthquake day.

Intuition/Mystery—While I was on Maui, I met a woman named Dee who worked at the activities desk of my condo. I followed my intuition to spend time with her and the conversations were full of magic and affirmation.

Bible Mothers for Ivy Celtic Moon Mother
    Old Testament – Rahab
    New Testament – The Unnamed Woman
                with the Issue of Blood

Ivy Bible Mother—Old Testament
Rahab

Scripture: Joshua 2:1-14, 6:20-22, 25

Then Joshua son of Nun secretly sent two spies from Shittim. "Go, look over the land," he said, "especially Jericho." So they went and entered the house of a prostitute name Rahab and stayed there.

The king of Jericho was told, "Look! Some of the Israelites have come to her tonight to spy out the land." So the king of Jericho sent this message to Rahab: "Bring out the men who came to you and entered your house, because they have come to spy out the whole land."

But the woman had taken the two men and hidden them. She said, "Yes, the men came to me, but I did not know where they had come from. At dusk, when it was time to close the city gate, the men left. I don't know which way they went. Go after them quickly. You may catch up with them." (But she had taken them up to the roof and hidden them under stalks of flax men had laid out on the roof.) So the men set out in pursuit of the spies on the road that leads to the fords of the Jordan, and as soon as the pursuers were gone out, the gate was shut.

Before the spies lay down for the night, she went up on the roof and said to them, "I know that the Lord has given this land to you and that a great fear of you has fallen on us, so that all who live in this country are melting in fear because of you. We have heard how the Lord dried up the water out of the Red Sea for you when you came out of Egypt, and what you did to Sihon and Og, the two kings of the Amorites east of the Jordan, whom you completely destroyed. When we heard of it, our hearts melted and everyone's courage failed because of you, for the Lord your God is God in heaven above and on the earth below. Now then, please swear to me by the Lord that you will show kindness to my family, because I have shown kindness to you. Give me a sure sign that you will spare the lives of my father and mother, my brothers and sisters, and all who belong to them, and that you will save us from death."

"Our lives for your lives!" the men assured her. "If you don't tell what we are doing, we will treat you kindly and faithfully when the Lord gives us the land."

When the trumpets sounded, the people shouted, and at the sound of the trumpet, when the people gave a loud shout, the wall collapsed; so every man charged straight in, and they took the city. They devoted the city to the Lord and destroyed with the sword every living thing in it – men and women, young and old, cattle, sheep and donkeys.

Joshua said to the two men who had spied on the land, "Go into the prostitute's house and bring her out and all who belong to her, in accordance to your oath to her.

Joshua spared Rahab the prostitute, with her family and all who belonged to her, because she hid the men Joshua had sent as spies to Jericho – and she lives among the Israelites to this day

Interpretation

Rahab is an ancestor of Jesus, and yet, has been considered by some to be a "black sheep" within the family tree. After all, which of the Christian Church leaders have told us that Jesus was the descendent of a woman who was considered a prostitute? As Herbert Lockyer points out in *Women of the Bible,* three times Rahab is referred to as a harlot.

Rahab was of the Amorite Tribe in Jericho. We all know the old story of "Joshua fought the battle of Jericho," but we don't often hear of the role Rahab played in that victory. As noted by Helen Bruch Pearson in *Mother Roots,* this spy story is a woman's story – Rahab's story. She was approached by two of Joshua's spies and, following her intuition, chose to hide them from their pursuers. Not only did she hide the spies, she also was willing to state her price for their protection.

As Irene Nowell explains in *Women in the Old Testament,* her faith and intuition is manifested not just in her words, but in her deeds. Imagine if that act had not happened. Jesus is her direct descendent. Instead, her actions resulted in the protection of her family in the fall of Jericho and demonstrated her willingness to embrace her destiny and follow her intuition.

Ivy Bible Mother—New Testament
Unnamed Woman with the Issue of Blood

Scripture: Mark 5:25-34

And a woman was there who had been subject to bleeding for twelve years. She had suffered a great deal under the care of many doctors and had spent all she had, yet instead of getting better she grew worse. When she heard about Jesus, she came up behind him in the crowd and touched his cloak, because she thought, "If I just touch his clothes, I will be healed." Immediately the bleeding stopped and she felt in her body that she was freed from her suffering.

At once Jesus realized that power had gone out of him. He turned around in the crowd and asked, "Who touched my clothes?"

"You see the people crowding against you," his disciples answered, "and yet you ask, 'Who touched me?'"

But Jesus kept looking around to see who had done it. Then the woman, knowing what had happened to her, came and fell at his feet and, trembling with fear, told him the whole truth. He said to her, "Daughter, your faith has healed you. Go in peace and be freed from your suffering."

Interpretation

This is a woman who was considered permanently unclean since her flow had continued nonstop for 12 years. She had seen many doctors, and had received no relief. Imagine what that must have been like in a time prior to sanitary napkins and tampons. No one had been able to give this woman relief, and she was shunned by her entire community. Nell W. Mahoney imagines her life in *From Mary to Lydia* as one of outcast and loneliness. She was unable to attend social functions or temple, and her husband was not allowed to touch her.

She had heard rumors of this prophet, Jesus, and his ability to heal people. Then she heard that Jesus was actually coming to her village. In *Women of the Bible,* she could not publicly throw herself at Jesus' feet and ask for healing. She was unclean, and therefore, unwelcome within the village.

In *Women in the New Testament,* we understand the woman built her confidence by talking to herself and finally, in seeing Jesus pass near her, had the courage as well as the **intuition** and faith to reach out and touch the hem of his garment as he passed. She was, in her action, immediately healed. Jesus felt the power leave as it filled her and turned to ask who had touched him. She stepped forward and explained her action. Jesus respectfully told her, "Your faith has healed you."

Ivy Bible Mother Meditation
Rahab and Unnamed Woman with the Issue of Blood

You are seated in a quiet space with the deep color of blue night all around you. Visualize an anchor of light coming from the top of your head down through your feet and hooking into the core of the earth. Breathe deeply sending energy down this cord and see it coming back up into your being.

Your space is open to the sky and you can see the stars twinkling above you. As you look into the distance, there are two women heading toward you. They walk slowly and confidently in the night air. They join you sitting on the ground and each in turn look deeply into your eyes. Their gazes are quiet and confident. One pair of eyes is hazel in color and a bit defiant. The other pair is a deep brown, and carries a sense of quiet determination. These are the Bible Mothers of Still Movement. They come to you and work with you to help you to trust your inner knowing, trust the silence and know when silence will transform into action.

The three of you, together, begin a time of observation. Begin to feel the ebb and flow of your own body, your inner voice and its messages. Allow these Bible Mothers to accompany you on that inner journey of discovery and invite them into your daily living patterns. Rahab brings for you a golden light she places in your forehead. Our Unnamed Woman brings a warm red glow she places in your abdomen. Feel the energy begin to flow first from your forehead down into the abdomen and then mix and flow back up to your head. As the flow continues, expand it from your abdomen down your legs and arms.

Allow the energy to pour out of you creating a bubble of energy embracing you. Breathe in the clear energy. Enjoy the sensation created in this still moment and bask a bit before returning to your room.

Rahab and The Unnamed Woman
with the Issue of Blood Worksheet

1. When these women came up to you, who did you see? Did you recognize them?

2. How did it feel to be in stillness with them? What did you feel?

3. How did you experience your own ebb and flow?

4. How did the energy flow from the abdomen to head and through your body? Did you experience any blockages? Where were the blockages? Were you able to clear them?

Tina Carey

Images of Bible Mothers
Rahab and The Unnamed Woman
with the Issue of Blood

Key Word Journal for Bible Mothers
Rahab and The Unnamed Woman
with the Issue of Blood

Key Words of Empowerment

- Mystery
- Stillness
- Intrigue
- Intuition
- Rhythm
- Balance

REED ✦ NGETAL

Reed Celtic Moon Mother

She reflects power, passion, agitation, clearing and the power to retrieve your soul. The flaming eye reminds you to stay alert as you cleanse through the fire of anger. It also contains within it the expression of spirit rising from the depths of your darkness. The web is a reminder that no matter how far away you believe you are from Spirit, others and even yourself, everything is interlinked and therefore, nothing is lost. The Spider reminds you of the power to weave, create new patterns and communicate your truth. Reed is the Celtic Moon Mother who brings about deep transformation whether you like it or not! She comes in the fall, in the time of Scorpio when the nights become very long and our days are shortened.

Time of Year

Reed reflects the sun angled at Scorpio and tipping into Sagittarius. She radiates her moonbeams throughout the Celtic celebration of Samhain.

Key Words of Empowerment

- Power, Passion,
- Agitation, Clearing
- Power of soul retrieval
- Endings, death and rebirth
- Soul protection

Personal Inspiration

Endings, death, rebirth—Reed is a tough time of the year. It is during this time that we are invited to totally clear out all our old beliefs and prepare our souls for rebirth. Just like farmers need to clear the land in the fall to prepare the soil for planting, we have the opportunity during the time of Reed to reflect on our own lives to clear out that which no longer serves us. Consider it like "raking the leaves" of our inner selves – creating the pile and then either shoveling it out or burning the pile to ash. Sometimes the soul preparation comes through anger, sometimes through grief or a combination of anger and grief. It is through these painful processes that transformation and rebirth begins.

Clearing—Reflecting on Reed during 2001, I released a lot of old relationships and the anger that remained particularly with the men in my life. These releases took place during meditations.

One method is to go into meditation and visualize guides and angels surrounding us in a protective circle. Then visualize opening our spiritual body. Look at what bonds are on our spiritual body attached to this person. Sometimes I see thick cords or telephone wires for example. Ask for the cords to be released with grace and ease.

Visualize the perfect tool to cut these ties – it may be a knife, or scissors or even an axe. Once the ties are totally cleared, visualize white light closing the spiritual body. Thank the guides and angels for their help and that's it. I repeat the ritual for seven days. Each day brings a new visualization for the bonds – they get smaller/thinner every day until they are barely visible. Cutting the ties allows me to release the anger and the relationships.

Agitation—An example of recognizing the power of anger was when I went to visit my stepsister, Ginna Sue, to do some hands on-healing. She had colon cancer. My realization was that her cancer had manifested due to an inability to express her anger. I realized that I had a similar pattern as well.

Endings/Soul Protection—In 2002, my experience of Reed was that of a tragedy. My nephew, Greg Smith, was killed in a car accident on Thanksgiving. He left a young wife and son. This tragic incident certainly changed my life as well as the life of my entire family. His sudden death allowed a very deep transformation as the family bonded through a shared loss. For example, in addition to family and friends attending his memorial in California, merchants near our bookstore as well as customers joined us. This tragedy provided an opportunity for the community to come together in support of my sister and our family.

Bible Mothers for Reed Celtic Moon Mother
Old Testament – Deborah
New Testament – Pilate's Wife

Tina Carey

Reed Bible Mother -- Old Testament
Deborah

Scripture: Judges 4:4-18, 21-22

Deborah, a prophetess, the wife of Lappidoth, was leading Israel at that time. She held court under the Palm of Deborah between Ramah and Bethel in the hill country of Ephraim, and the Israelites came to her to have their disputes decided. She sent for Barak, son of Abinoam from Kedesh in Naphtali and said to him, "The Lord, the God of Israel commands you." 'Go, take with you ten thousand men of Naphtali and Zebulun and lead the way to Mount Tabor. I will lure Sisera, the commander of Jabin's army, with his chariots and his troops to the Kishon River and give him into your hands.'"

Barak said to her, "If you go with me, I will go; but if you don't go with me, I won't go."

"Very well," Deborah said, "I will go with you. But because of the way you are going about this, the honor will not be yours, for the Lord will hand Sisera over to a woman." So Deborah went with Barak to Kedesh, where he summoned Zebulun and Naphtali. Ten thousand men followed him, and Deborah also went with him.

Now Heber the Kenite had left the other Kenites, the descendents of Hobab, Moses' brother-in-law, and pitched his tent by the great tree in Zaanannim near Kedesh.

When they told Sisera that Batrak son of Abinoam had gone up to Mount Tabor, Sisera gathered together his nine hundred iron chariots and all the men with him, from Harosheth Haggoyim to the Kishon River.

Then Deborah said to Barak, "Go! This is the day the Lord has given Sisera into your hands. Has not the Lord gone ahead of you?" So Barak went down Mount Tabor, followed by ten thousand men. At Barak's advance, the Lord routed Sisera and all his chariots and army as far as Harosheth Haggoyim. All the troops of Sisera fell by the sword; not a man was left.

Sisera, however, fled on foot to the tent of Jael, the wife of Heber the Kenite, because there were friendly relations between Jabin king of Hazor and the clan of Heber the Kenite.

Jael went out to meet Sisera and said to him, "Come, my lord, come right in. Don't be afraid." So he entered her tent and she put covering over him.

But Jael, Heber's wife, picked up a tent peg and a hammer and went quietly to him while he lay fast asleep, exhausted. She drove the peg through his temple into the ground, and he died.

Barak came by in pursuit of Sisera, and Jael went out to meet him. "Come," she said, "I will show you the man you're looking for." So he went in with her, and there lay Sisera with the tent peg through his temple – dead.

From the Song of Deborah

In the days of Shamgar son of Anath,

In the days of Jael, the roads were abandoned;

Travelers took to winding paths.

Village life in Israel ceased

Ceased until I, Deborah arose,

Arose a mother in Israel

When they chose new gods,

War came to the city gates

And not a shield or spear was seen

Among forty thousand in Israel

My heart is with Israel's princes,

With the willing volunteers among the people.

Praise the Lord.

Then the people of the Lord

Went down to the city gates.

Wake up, wake up, Deborah!

Wake up, wake up, break out in song!

Interpretation

Deborah was a strong, forceful leader of the people. She was a prophetess and a judge. Herbert Lockyer in *The Women of the Bible* describes Deborah as the woman who was a fearless patriot. He notes that like Joan of Arc, Deborah was similarly gifted with superior spiritual, mental and physical powers to lead her people and leave her mark on the history of her people. Through her own warrior nature, she brought deep transformation for her people.

As noted by Irene Nowell in *Women in the Old Testament*, Deborah was one of the heroes described in the book of Judges. She is a poet, a prophetess and a judge. She is powerful and she knows it.

Her people had been cruelly oppressed by their enemies for many years and were hungry for redemption and a path out. Deborah spoke of God's word and purpose and when asked, helped lead her people into battle. She led those people since Barak was unwilling to venture out without her – even though he had been commanded by God to do so.

We are given a true **death** and **rebirth** story here in the Israelite journey. This is the story of their own death into oppression and rebirth under the leadership of Deborah, a strong warrioress, a prophetess and judge.

Reed Bible Mother—New Testament
Pilate's Wife

Scripture: Matthew 27:19

While Pilate was sitting on his judge's seat, his wife sent him this message: "Don't have anything to do with that innocent man, for I have suffered a great deal today in a dream because of him."

When Pilate saw that he was getting nowhere, but that instead an uproar was starting, he took water and washed his hands in front of the crowd. "I am innocent of this man's blood," he said. "It is your responsibility!"

Interpretation

As I thought of the strength and **passion** of the transformation brought during the time of Reed, I struggled to find a woman in the New Testament. The Old Testament is full of stories of revenge and ripe with potential Bible Mothers. I was inspired to remember another unnamed woman who foretold great transformation – Pilate's wife.

Herbert Lockyer in *Women in the Bible* tells us that although Pilate's wife remains unnamed in the gospels, she is known as Claudia Procula, granddaughter of Emperor Augustus in *The Gospel of Nicodemus* one of the Apocryphal books. It is said that she was among the women of the higher classes who respected the Jewish faith.

This is a woman of Rome who had her own spiritual awakening in the form of an alarming and warning dream strong enough to shake her into action and to warn her husband with her note. Her dream was an incubator for the **death and rebirth** to come through the crucifixion of Jesus. As noted by Mary Ann Getty-Sullivan in *Women of the New Testament,* she tried to influence Pilate to judge in favor of justice versus injustice.

Imagine her fear in waking to such an image, and her premonition of the guilt that would follow her husband throughout eternity from this one action. Her courage comes in her willingness to speak her truth. In the story we see Pilate's attempt to redeem himself of the decision by "washing his hands" of the issue of Jesus.

Reed Bible Mother Meditation
Deborah and Pilate's Wife

You are seated in a fully dark space. It is the darkest part of the night. Visualize an anchor of light coming from the top of your head down through your feet and hooking into the core of the earth. Breathe deeply sending energy down this cord and see it coming back up into your being.

As you begin to focus on your breath, you notice two women standing in front of you. They are tall and stately and their robes are black in color with red veils on their faces. These women come forward to you. Deborah is on the left and she carries a book of spiritual law for you. Pilate's wife on the right brings you a basin of holy water to wash your hands before your journey. These women will be your guides as you walk your path of transformation.

Once you have washed, take the book of Law and place it into an inner pocket in your cloak. Allow these women to raise you up and walk with you toward a distant glen. It is night as you arrive and there is a crescent moon in the sky which provides just enough light to illuminate your path.

Once you reach the glen, you are invited to stand next to a tall tree. Deborah and Pilate's wife will stand on either side of the tree as you continue your journey. You see a bit of clearing just ahead, and within this open space, there is a small garden needing tending. This is your garden of dreams. Notice which plants are ready to be picked and where your weeding needs to be done. Tend your garden and allow the pruning to take place. Water is provided for your work as well as any tools you require.

Spend as much time here as you feel necessary to clear out all the old growth and allow space for the new. Note that your Bible Mothers are with you through this time. When you are done, come back to the tree and allow the women to escort you back to your room.

Deborah and Pilate's Wife Worksheet

1. When Deborah and Pilate's wife approached you, who did you see? Did you recognize them?

2. As you entered your garden, what type of plants grew there?

3. What condition was the garden in?

4. What needed weeding?

Tina Carey

Images of Bible Mothers
Deborah and Pilate's Wife

Key Word Journal for Bible Mothers
Deborah and Pilate's Wife

Key Words of Empowerment

- Power, Passion,
- Agitation, Clearing
- Power of soul retrieval
- Endings, death and rebirth
- Soul protection

ELDER ✦ RUIS

©1997 Katherine Torres, Ph. D., Transpersonal Development

Elder Celtic Moon Mother

She conveys the silent respect of sacredness. Her silver swirls reflect the moon's ability to take you to the door of your Higher Self and the Higher Power of the Universe through the pathway of ease and flow. Her face encourages the feeling of silent repose. Her blue eyes represent peacefulness and clarity brought forth through silence.

Time of Year

Elder reflects the time of Sagittarius moving into Capricorn.

Key Words of Empowerment

- Silent respect of sacredness
- Quiet after the storm
- Healing, inner hearing
- Initiation
- Receiving
- Mystical wisdom

Personal Inspiration

Healing/Inner hearing—Elder comes at Christmas time and brings with her an invitation to be silent – to listen to the small still voice within. During the time of Elder, many times I had a lot changing in my personal life. I did regular meditations during this time. One night I had a dream where I gave birth. There were two women and one man attending me and they took the child, a girl. I reminded them that I alone was to feed her since I would be nursing her. They brought her back to me and she was much smaller than my real children when they were born. I noticed a birth mark on the baby that led me to believe that I had given birth to a new me. I saw this dream as a reflection of the deep inner work and my own spiritual rebirth as I continued to grow and change.

Silent respect for sacredness—In 2002, we celebrated Christmas without my nephew, Greg who I previously mentioned had been killed in a car accident. We held his memorial on December 28th and I found myself in a space of preparation that led me to a day of silent introspection. His memorial was an amazing experience and a testament to his spirit as well as to the support for my sister from our community.

Initiation—In 2005, I traveled to Belgium during the time of Elder to become a Dame in the Order of St. Stanislas, a true initiation. This is an initiation similar to being "knighted." Being a female, the Prince didn't use a sword to acknowledge me; instead he placed his hand on my head for a blessing. I spent that week in the presence of a wonderful male friend and thoroughly enjoyed the opportunity to explore a new city as well as experience this initiation in the physical as well as the spiritual realm. The trip brought opportunity for reflection and my recognition that I miss being married.

Bible Mothers for Elder Celtic Moon Mother

New Testament – Hannah

Old Testament – Phoebe

Elder Bible Mother—Old Testament
Hannah

Scripture: 1 Samuel 1:2, 8-13, 19-20

He had two wives; one was called Hannah and the other Peninnah. Peninnah had children but Hannah had none.

And because the Lord had closed her womb, her rival kept provoking her in order to irritate her. This went on year after year. Whenever Hannah went up to the house of the Lord, her rival provoked her till she wept and would not eat. Elkannah, her husband would say to her, "Hannah, why are you weeping? Why don't you eat? Why are you downhearted? Don't I mean more to you than ten sons?"

Once when they had finished eating and drinking in Shiloh, Hannah stood up. Now Eli the priest was sitting on a chair by the doorpost of the Lord's temple. In bitterness of her soul Hannah wept much and prayed to the Lord. And she made a vow, saying, "O Lord Almighty, if you will look upon your servant's misery and remember me, and not forget your servant but give her a son, then I will give him to the Lord for all the days of his life, and no razor will ever be used on his head."

As she kept on praying to the Lord, Eli observed her mouth. Hannah was praying in her heart, and her lips were moving but her voice was not heard.

Elhankah lay with Hannah his wife, and the Lord remembered her. So in the course of time Hannah conceived and gave birth to a son. She named him Samuel, saying, "Because I asked the Lord for him."

Interpretation

Herbert Lockyer in *Women in the Bible* describes Hannah as "the woman who personifies ideal motherhood." This is fascinating since Hannah has been barren. She is the favorite wife and has been unable to conceive.

This is the story of a woman so desperate for a child that she prays to God in silence, in her heart, searching for great healing. In her day, being barren was truly a disgrace. She had a tremendous willingness to go into her own inner temple to beseech God for a healing. Lockyer describes an inner serenity she embodied.

Irene Nowell in *Women in the Old Testament* describes Hannah's silent prayer as the first example of the tradition of private prayer. This is the first story of someone coming to a shrine simply to speak to God from her heart. Her healing was great in body and spirit. She gave Samuel to the Lord and subsequently gave birth to three sons and two daughters. Samuel went on to become a priest, and a prophet serving God.

Hannah was disciplined in her life and willing to listen within. Her silence prepared her for her initiation into motherhood and the sacrifice of giving her first born back to the God, who had given him to her.

Elder Bible Mother— New Testament
Phoebe

Scripture: Romans 16:1-2

I commend to you our sister Phoebe, a servant of the church in Cenchrea. I ask you to receive her in the Lord in a way worthy of the saints and to give her any help she may need from you, for she has been a great help to many people, including me.

Interpretation

Herbert Lockyer states in *Women of the Bible* that Phoebe is the woman who wore the badge of kindness. Phoebe took the responsibility of bringing Paul's letter to Rome. It began as a simple and convenient assignment. As she began her travels, she used her time to cultivate her own time of sacred silence.

Phoebe is spoken as a woman of strong faith and as noted by Lockyer wore the "light of the world" well. She was well traveled in her own right and was inspired by the message of Paul—the message of the teachings of Jesus.

Mary Ann Getty-Sullivan describes her as one of the early female traveling missionaries. Phoebe used her travel time to go within, listen to that soft voice and cultivate a period of healing before her arrival in Rome. This time alone provided time and discipline to rest before the true tasks would begin.

Elder Bible Mother Meditation
Hannah and Phoebe

You are seated in a space of dim light just as dawn begins to break. Visualize an anchor of light coming from the top of your head down through your feet and hooking into the core of the earth. Breathe deeply sending energy down this cord and see it coming back up into your being.

You see two women approaching you in the dim light. These women join you in total silence. They come forward to lead you keeping their eyes down. They are full of peace and have come to witness your time in sacred silence with the Great Mother. Know that even in your Silence, you remain a part of all of us.

You are led to a soft chair and seated. Sink into the softness and relax. Close your eyes and let the peaceful silence begin to fill you. Allow the thoughts in your head to become like waves on the beach. Let them subside into the distance and simply breathe. As you find that silent space, you will begin to hear a message within. Know that it is true.

You have the opportunity to respond and bring that message into your consciousness. Follow your instructions and come back to your self and your soft chair. Allow Phoebe and Hannah to greet you and present you with their special gifts of the spirit. Let them bring you back to your room.

Hannah and Phoebe Worksheet

1. *As Hannah and Phoebe approached you, did you recognize them? If so, who do they resemble?*

2. *As you sat down in your chair, what thoughts came into your mind?*

3. *As you relaxed, what message came from within?*

4. *What will you do with the message?*

Images of Bible Mothers
Hannah and Phoebe

Key Word Journal for Bible Mothers
Hannah and Phoebe

Key Words of Empowerment

- Silent respect of sacredness
- Quiet after the storm
- Healing, inner hearing
- Initiation
- Receiving
- Mystical wisdom

Acknowledgements

My life has been a fascinating series of events as I have walked this path of the Divine Feminine. I have many to thank:

- Cheryl Phillips for her persistent and loving support through my spiritual growth period.
- Katherine Torres for her *Daughters of the Moon* program and her kind and constant mentoring.
- Eileen Richardson for just "kicking me in the butt" to actually get this written.
- Cheryl Russell, my fabulous editor for her vision of the potential for this work.
- My daughter, Ali Carey, for being a reflection of me in the world.
- My sisters, Carole Smith, Cathy Schumm, Mary Schwartz, Sharon Fehring and Ginna Ruggles.
- My dear girlfriends who have helped along the way.

I have a number of men who have been a gift in my life and have also contributed to this effort:

- My sons, Sean and Ryan Carey and Eugene Liu, have created rich opportunities for me to see possibilities for themselves and for me.
- Steve Carey, my creative partner in this endeavor has been willing to share his gift of painting in the cover of this book and a bit of himself in this journey.
- Brad Harmer has been my "personal knight," supportive of my journey and a steadfast friend.

Printed in the United States
87206LV00002B/139-168/A

9 781432 705411